MY HEART IN YOUR HANDS
Poems from Namibia

Compiled by
Naitsikile Iizyenda
and
Jill Kinahan

UNAM
PRESS
UNIVERSITY OF NAMIBIA

University of Namibia Press
www.unam.edu.na/unam-press
unampress@unam.na
Private Bag 13301
Windhoek
Namibia

First published: 2020
Cover design: Nambowa Malua
Design and layout: Jigsaw Graphic Design & Layout

ISBN 978-99916-42-57-4

Supported by the National Arts Council of Namibia

Distribution
In Namibia by Namibia Book Market: www.namibiabooks.com
Internationally by the African Books Collective: www.africanbookscollective.com

CONTENTS

INTRODUCTION

My heart in your hands is the extraordinary result of calling on poets in Namibia to speak, of promising them a publishing platform.

Since the inception of the University of Namibia Press in 2011, poets have submitted their work for consideration in spite of our declared position that we did not publish poetry. The gentle insistence of these submissions gradually eroded the banks of our defences, and in 2018 we published two anthologies: *Hakahana* by Hugh Ellis (a revised edition) and *Ancestors and Other Visitors* by Don Stevenson. These were individual collections published with a very small print run but they added to the small body of Namibian poems available for academic study. Their publication was supported by Professor Jairos Kangira, a member of our Editorial Board and lifelong lecturer in English literature, who urged us to publish Namibian literature for the curriculum. Also a member of the Editorial Board, and, as a lecturer in poetry with a vested interest, Dr Nelson Mlambo told us that what was needed was a multi-authored anthology which would give "more variety, more flavour, appeal, craft and form" (in litt. Mlambo, 2.06.2017).

Around this time, Deputy Director Ms M'kariko Amagulu, representing the National Arts Council of Namibia, approached us with the idea of a partnership in publishing. What better project than an anthology of Namibian poetry? We agreed to conceptualise a volume and prepare it for publication, and the Arts Council would support its printing.

After much internal discussion, we decided to put out a national call and open our arms to all poets, new and established, for unpublished poems on any and all things Namibian, in any of the Namibian languages. We wanted to be open and inclusive, and our aim was to encourage new poets and provide an opportunity for established poets to share new work. We wanted to showcase writers whom we believed would continue to produce great work. We asked for well-crafted poems that employed skilful and imaginative use of language, metre and rhyme, and experimented with texture and form. We wanted conscious, thought-provoking poetry which generated questions.

What a response we received! The poets exceeded these requirements, employing innovative form and style, and imaginative use of everyday experience to create immediacy, symbolism and imagery. Over 400 poems flooded in, including 47 in various local languages, and in spite of an extension, entries continued to flow in well past the deadline. We had opened the floodgates of creativity and stood on the banks watching with wonder, and when we started to read those poems, we were alternately elated, dismayed, humbled, disgusted, uplifted and charmed. We had opened our arms, but the poets had opened their hearts.

We selected 120 for review. As a scholarly press, we assess even poets' heart-work in order to keep to our brief and retain international academic standards. We attempted to turn this process into an educational exercise, a way of contributing to the poets' development because discourse sharpens and improves standards, but it proved to be too time-consuming to give detailed feedback even to 120 poets, let alone over 400. Most of the poems in the volume, however, have benefitted from commentary, editing, proof-reading and in some cases, revision by the poets themselves following feedback. We are most grateful to our three perceptive and encouraging reviewers, from Namibia, South Africa and the United Kingdom, whom, for the purposes of our double blind review process, we keep anonymous. At the back of the volume, we include a section giving brief biographies for the poets to show that they come from all walks of life, from professors to prisoners, and that creative and powerful expression trumps scholarship or grammatical competence in the writing of poetry.

Our initial enthusiasm for embracing all Namibian languages was not sustainable. The predominant language was English, with 17 poems in Afrikaans, ten in Oshiwambo, eight in Khoekhoegowab, six in German, four in Silozi and one each in Rukwangali and in Otjiherero. Our intention was to treat all languages the same, on an equal footing, but problems of equity soon arose: either we could not find expert reviewers in all the different languages to assess these poems in time for our deadlines, or, where we had reviewers, not all the poems were approved for publication at tertiary level. We did not want to have different standards for poems in the different languages, and we also did not want a markedly small number of indigenous language poems. Our solution was to continue to work on the poems and to view *My heart in your hands* as the first of many anthologies to come.

The title for the anthology is a quotation from the poem on the back cover of Rupi Kaur's volume *Milk and Honey* (Andrews McMeel Publishing, 2014). That poem is a fair reflection of the content of this collection: a journey of surviving, the blood, sweat and tears, the hurting, the loving, the breaking and the possible healing.

And in your hand you hold the hearts of nearly 100 poets who have, with courage, honesty, and love, driven by the creative impulse, spilled their thoughts, tears, rage, regrets, love and laughter onto the pages of this book. The most sensitive and most brutal of citizens, they have privileged us with a glimpse into the nation's soul. Hold this book gently.

Arising from the themes which the poets explored, we chose ten, and grouped the poems in the way in which we thought best deepened, developed, unfolded or contrasted the ideas expressed. The poems were so powerful, that when we had them grouped, lines from individual poems jumped out as obvious titles for each section. Appreciation of the uniqueness of our country's landscapes and life forms opens the volume, followed by equally heartfelt gratitude to our mothers. A cross-section of Namibian voices and characters from different cultures, backgrounds and social classes clamour for attention in the next section, showing the rich diversity, aspirations, successes and tragedies of our growing nation – oh, get to know us, joyful, banal, violent, thoughtful, eccentric, but above all, real, and full of life! The fourth section gets down to social criticism, exploring the underbelly of our society, bringing into the light issues which are normally silenced and hidden, while the next three sections explore depression, violence, and suicide and death more deeply. The poets highlight these serious social and personal ills, usually divulged only by statistics and factual reports while being regarded by ordinary people as matters of shame. The poets insist these concerns be scrutinised, felt, and understood in a personal perspective. Issues of inequality, racial hatred, poverty, injustice and genocide are raised in the subsequent section, unpacked as stark, authentic, ruthless. While questioning or fuming, our people are also unbelievably accepting. We are good at scrutinising our dark side, but we also love: even across the borders of foreign countries, we can feel we've come home; we love in the redemption of our faith, within unforgiving prison walls, in the voluptuous beauty of our land, the despair of what cannot be, and in our understated humour. In the final section, we glory in our Africanness, our traditions, our innovative playfulness, and our special identity as Namibians, with our "roots in the sand" (Sylvia Schlettwein, p. 146, this volume).

Changed forever by our journey into the poet's world, and richly rewarded, we wish you, the reader, to be equally transported by this work.

Naitsikile Iizyenda and Jill Kinahan
Windhoek
February, 2020

THE POEMS

WHERE THE OCEAN
AND
DESERT KISS

Only Namibian

I come from a country where the ocean and desert kiss
Beautiful piece of savannah and sky
I come from a people of warriors whose blood
Has watered my freedom
Idiom and
Tale. I have heard as child
Wild winds have carried spear
To the ear
Of those instructed to divide
My Namib soul by
Tongue and tribe.
Bantustan systems no longer stand
For I come from the north and south
Born of east and west
Have you seen?
My history
I am you and you are me
I am Namibian

Zemha Gawachas

clouds

I
what a mass of   nothingness
full of water   full of gas
lacking sheer solidity
dripping
        with humidity
building bulging breaking burst
making fertile   quenching thirst
strato
        alto
                cumulus
stormy striking thunderous
fast disguising sunny skies
making wet what drought heat dries

is it something   is it not
just a cold front   warming up
fast occluding   running dry
all exuding pouring sky
layered
                levelled
                        drifting past
trying hard to make it last
for the moments of solution
washing vanishing pollution

II
out of cloudy mist they grow
desert flowers' sandy flow
creeping out into the sun
opening petals showing fun
fast retracting in the bright
deep enclosing precious light
revelling in capsuled gleam
hypnotized in cloudy dream

III
Princess Flower of the sand
opening where clouds can land

Klaus Rennack

From ocean to desert

From the waves to the desert
there I find my peace
there my mind clears
In those moments the world slows down
They call it Skeleton Coast
yet there, I get life

When all around me
is crashing and clashing
I am guaranteed of an escape
a haven in an unexpected space
They call it lost and forsaken
yet there, I get life

When I cannot stand the sounds
and the air of modern life becomes too thick
I can find sweet silence there
I find the fresh salty air there
They call it deserted
yet there, I feel at home.

Hannah H. Tarindwa

Huab and Ugab

two rivers in their beds
they never get together
not in a million years –
though they are close
to be connected
and have a bonded
way of nature
of wildlife, tracks
of bush and trees –
in times of dryness
times of wetness
experience a common fate
they'll never meet
though they meander
from source to mouth
from south to north
they are so different
are familiar
are worlds apart
but congruent –
the only place
where they're concurrent
is Benguela – out at sea

Klaus Rennack

The Skeleton Coast

When he stepped into the night
All the mirages vanished
And it was his lucid reflections
That brought the realizations of virtues.
In this wilderness, one eyed monsters
Guard the shores of rocky coasts
Troubled seas are nobody's coasters
Heard of the *Deutscher* that slept and sunk?
Now deep bottom resting in Pisces
For on the surface skeletons surf
Fighting the current washing them ashore
Onto the coast of skeletons.

Welcome to the skeleton coast
Uninhabited yet many find cradle
Bones of all sorts of folks and those of whales
Sleep while the mist blankets the sun away.
These are no runaway souls
See how the seagulls guide ships.
Sailors are lured to the gate of Kunene
Where the waves pound a euphonic roar
And ships are mesmerized by the rococo.
As the ocean robs the treasures of pirates,
Iron termites nimbly turn ships to rust
While the desert lion looks on
With his majestic bronze mane
From the summit of Damaraland.

Sail these waters at your own peril
Sharks have abandoned its lethal tides
Untamed by the moon she defies nature.
Benguela, you are exquisitely beautiful
No make-up, no artificial beaches.
The curvatures on her coast are natural.
Her breath stinks with a seaweed breeze,
And in her eyes, exists no guilt.
Her tongue, she has drowned for garrison.
Seaman souls whisper at each sunrise
Hoping a passerby hears their distresses
lost in her wildly unkempt hair
It seems she harbours no heart.

Batchotep

Swells Smash Dias Point

Sit thrilled
Your back against the door
Of this incongruous old foghorn house
And feel
The rising bursts of spray
And salt-foam suck your gasping laugh
Sit tight
Atop your rock –
Apparent safety lies in height –
And watch
As mesmerising waves
Stalk unsuspecting you in droves.

Sit
Stripped of strength
Small pink and cringing thing
And shake
In icy fear and
Naked helplessness
And retch
Your heart into your mouth
As all the sea heaves up at microscopic you
In one
Magnificent monolithic monster of a wave
Advancing from and blotting out the west and half the sky

For NOW
You pink and cringing thing
You face the overwhelming ocean all alone
But you
Are not Canute or Christ
YOU ARE ME and if I wish to
STAY
This side of Timelessness
And miss the instant of extinction
ACT
As only feeble instinct
Moves one to react and that is FAST ...

And so the foghorn house
Is gone
And I unharmed by nature's threat
Thank instinct for my life
And God.

Crispin D. P. Clay

Riches in a Poor Country

Let me extol
the wealth of my soul...

     summer sunshine thickening the air with waves of melted brass,
     rippling beaten gold when the wind blows through dry grass,
     an iridescent patch of powdered rubies on a scarlet-breasted sunbird,
     a glint of garnet feathers on flamingos winging westward,
     acacia flowers in silken puffs in the warmth of springtime noons,
     cinnamon, paprika and nutmeg, piled into powdery dunes,
     a snake-breasted eagle sculptured in onyx and alabaster,
     silver-studded stars in an ebony eternity eternally growing vaster
          a pearlescent moon, a plush velvety night,
          an amethyst sea under crystallised light...

Thus I image my Africa to give it value in the eyes
Of those who set the standards for the wealthy and the wise,
When in fact the beauty of this land should be the original source and measure
Of all the much less worthy things the rest of the world seems to treasure.

     Veld-flowers are not jewels in the grass,
     Nor are the birds' wings gemmed.
     The African land has its own wild beauty
     Which cannot by tame metaphors ever be limned.

          Turn the comparisons inside out,
          Let raindrops be diamonds to no one,
          But praise the world's most exquisite diamond
          For shining like a raindrop under hot-white African sun.

Dianne Hubbard

Drought

Laboured and toiled
Till land boiled
Perhaps, burnt
Backbones bent

Hands rested on legs
Can't hold heads
Under shades of leaves
Aloof under eaves

Without rains
Immense pain
Cattle, goat, sheep dehydrate
Yearning and yawning for carbohydrate

Forefathers provide
Children abide
Cast away demons
Of this omen bemoaned

Sifiso Nyati

Praying Mantis

I stared into your eyes
cloudy water droplets each
a globe encapsulating
a fathomless
indigo
pinprick

Tiny crystal balls they were
protruding from opposite
sides of your head
reflecting back
nothing of my own image
but a delicate milky alertness
attentive to the song of the universe
and all within it.

Jacquie Tarr

ses fontein

first fountain for forward
for quenching some thirst
a mother's convention
in nurturing birth

next fountain for growing
for getting abreast
a young generation
with restless unrest

third fountain for grown-up
for going ahead
adult for confession
with water and bread

fourth fountain for reaching
for leaving behind
mature in religion
trustworthy we find

fifth fountain for fruitful
for coming of age
the richest progression
for leaving one's cage

sixth fountain for loving
for finishing fine
the deepest of waters
made for you alone

Klaus Rennack

Katutura

They will tell you that Katutura is too dangerous
that we were bred to be clothed with violence and stupidity
that we have nothing to offer but kneel
as we try to clean up the perfectly clean dirt of theirs.
They will tell you that womb shall realise its purpose
long before your voice is able to form words.
Katutura is the heart of their disappointment but that it is not what is to me:

It is a place where children's joy echoes from one street to another.
Where neighbours gossip with microphones yet still keep open secrets
silent.
Katutura breeds the bravest of hearts
the strongest of wills
and the most loveable people.
Katutura greets you with a friendly smile each day
never waves goodbye
and is always there.

Jacobina Kalunduka

Peace

Have you ever *listened* to the Peace of the World?
Have you ever felt it or watched its hues?
    Not as a screech from a mindless mob
    Nor a meaningless manhandled word in the news

       BUT

Peace in the ear as the sand-dunes moan
As the south-west wind sings a wild refrain;
Peace in the smell of the fog-washed air
As the mist tumbles up and away into blue;
Peace in the grumble and swish of the surf
As it flops in a furl of white onto green
Onto white onto smooth stretching reaches of beach.

Peace in the burst of a broadside of tide
As it shatters to spray in a spout from the swell;
Peace in the sun setting fire to the dunes
In the distance and closer to saltpans and spume;
Peace in the weaving of wings in the wind
In the wave of a cormorant vee over sea
As it dips in a flick for a sip as it glides.

Peace in the stillness of dunes in the dark
With the whisper and ripple of sand in a slide
Like the sound of a breeze through distant trees;
Peace in the eye as the sand sea and sky
Expand in the mind to the reaches of time
And the soul is alone where alone is All One.

Crispin D. P. Clay

MOTHERS
OF
NAMIBIA

Lady Mukwahepo

When emotions swelled up in your soul
Your tears inspired a revolution
Your tears sent your sons on a path
On a path to freedom
On a path of free thought

Your tears broke your daughters out of bondage
Your tears nourished a legion of fierce women
Your tears invoked a sense of justice
Your tears liberated a nation

Mercy George

The mothers of Namibia

The mothers of Namibia cried,
       for their children,
       for their husbands,
       for their freedom.
       They were helpless.
       They moved no-one.

But we now, are free.

The mothers of Africa are crying,
       to still the hollow laughter,
       to stop the bullets,
       to fill stomachs.
       They are in despair
       and reaching no-one.

But we now, are free.

The mothers of the world are moaning,
       their weeping sound
       in UN halls,
       in the ears of tyrants,
       they protest in songs.
       No-one is listening.

But we now, are free.

Our mothers and sisters wept
      for their babies,
      for the dead,
      for their fathers,
      for our prisoners.
      They moved no-one.

But we now, are free.

Then why do tears still form behind broken hands
      in Pakistan, in Europe,
      in Asia, in America, in Africa
      dropping on
      bloody floors,
      staining cheap newspaper pages

When we now, are free?

Pedro Vorster

Mother

I know not why you're sad, dear Mom
Don't cry a million tears for me!
For I am keen to leave this sac
And burst into this world you fear

You only see the hurt and toil
That saddens and makes people wail
You dread I will not ever see
Animals, trees and perfect skies

But I am keen to arrive soon
To play in oceans; laugh under suns
I want to love your cruel world,
know joy of family and friends

We children do have perfect dreams
in these seeming empty eyes
Look into mine, I beg you Mom …
You'll see how kind the world can be.

I know there's hope for this cruel world!
You just believe and carry me through.

Bronwen A Beukes

There is depth in Mommy's strength

I keep testing my mother's strength
And I'm scared she'll sag beneath my yoke.

I need my mother so much still –

But she's our mother, so I stand her off
To my saplings.
Though I am of age I wilt when exposed
To harsh settings.

I need her warmth still –

I yearn to be home but we're all set out; rooted apart.
With mommy as our only common; it's gloom.
But I'll uptake all nourishment to bloom.
And bare her flowers (and fruits)
Of infinite colours (and shoots).
I wish to sustain her laughter but I'm sad and mad.

I need my mother's tending still –

But she's weary from past tending yielding nothing.
Tender of gardeners, I hope to know my mother's strength
As not to 'push it'.
I hope to be home someplace else; well rooted as mommy had intended.
I hope for her to have breath to find me and live lavishly off me.
Alas, when she dies – I'll carry forth all of her memories.

And I hope my saplings to be of even depth, so collectively –
We'll pass on our mommy's strength.

Anne-Marie Issa Brown Garises

Tornado (or, The Only Poem You Ever Wrote)

tornado

(noun)

/tawr-ney-doh/

1.

A violently destructive windstorm characterised by a rotating column of air in contact with the surface of the Earth.

2.

The only poem you ever wrote, the pyramid that grief built.

Rémy Ngamije

Scrambling out of bed dressing quickly and then running out of the apartment forgetting to lock up
and running down the stairs fumbling the car keys the car coughing like its about to die and and oh
my god do not think of that death Jesus take the wheel fuck you are not even a believer but death
the drive to the hospital skipping the red lights and swerving the car into the parking lot and then
forgetting to put on the handbrake and the car bumping into the wall behind it and then you
are running into the reception calling that simple childish word that echoes for all eternity
Mamma! Mamma! Mamma! And the person at the reception does not know and then
you are told that she must be in the ER and then you are running running through
the brightly lit halls and then the corner where you bump into the nurse and
then the swearing because you are trying to find the corridor that leads
to the room where they save lives and surely this is the place where
they save lives otherwise what the fuck are hospitals for and this
is just the worst fucking thing that has ever happened and then
there is the room and there is the bed and oh my god oh my
god oh my god and oh my god and oh my god and you
pull back the curtain and it is the wrong bed and then
there is your father peeking from behind a curtain
and your brother as well and then the walk that
stumbles and the man is crying and the boy is
also crying but you are not crying just yet
but this is about to change and here
you are and there it is the bed the
real bed this time not the wrong
bed but you wish it was not
the real bed but fuck this
is the real bed and here
you are and there she
is and no this cannot
be her it is not her
it is not it is not
it is not her it
is not her it
is not her
it is not
her it
is

Unconditional Love (a letter to my mother)

The kind of pain you have endured
And continue to endure for us
I will never understand

You hurt so we don't have to
You starve so we can eat
You cry so we don't have to
You burn so we have heat
And we will never understand

In a world where people constantly choose themselves,
You continually choose us
And we will never understand

Gloria Ndilula

Dear Mamma

You hosted me for nine moonshines,
And gave me piggy-back for a dozen more.
I was moulded at your service,
And acclimatized to life on your lap.
Who could have done more?
I have no words to convey my heart,
Nor fair enough action to demonstrate it,
Even tears fall too short.
From above may you receive abundant felicity,
And keep fettle as your flesh mellows.
Forever I shall remember your copious tenderness,
For always my cradle days I shall cherish
As our unity I blissfully call to mind.

Job Ndeutapo Nghipandulwa

For Future Generations

We toil for the next generation.
So that what we hold dear to ourselves
And the value of what is most precious to us,
Will be received by them;
Even just a glimpse, if it reaches them filtered.
Maybe it will all go to one
Maybe it will go to all.
Yet we strive for a carry-over of legacies.
Legacies those that lived before us never imagined would be principle,
Never imagined would be seed,
Never imagined would grow into trees not to be called figs;
Because we bear much, and we bear lasting.
For one if not for all, or at least most.
So we toil.
Let these whips lash our backs if it means them laying
Peacefully on their backs;
Painless. Unharmed.
Undaunted. Free.
May they grow to know we saw their days before their eyes ever opened,
And thought of their lives before they even knew they had them.
If we don't succeed may they be our extension;
To carry on if not to complete.
To toil for their next generation.

Julia N.T. Nekomba

BORN
OF THE
TREE OF LIFE

African child!

African child!
Where are you?

African child!
What are you called?

African child!
Have you looked up to the sky lately?
Have you spoken to the sun and whispered to the moon?

African child!
Have you watched the liquid of life lately?
Seen it smile?
Inviting you to be invigorated?

African child!
Have you seen your brothers lately?
Big ear elephant?
Your brother with one horn?
And the golden one they call king?

African child!
Have you seen your aunt camelthorn?
Your uncle baobab?
I have heard them cry,
that their children are mean.

African child!
Whatever they call you,
of whatever hue
Wherever you are
You are a star
born of the tree of life
Shine your light on life

Aristides 'Are' Sambiliye

Man of My Life

The first time I met the man of my life
was in my mother's house.
It was love at first sight!
Not because we were struck by Cupid's arrows…
No! It was more than that.
His love was born long before I was born.
I still hadn't the faintest idea what love was
but the Man of My Life himself
was love personified.
The man of my Life himself
is pure love in its human form.

He dreaded that I was so tiny and helpless.
In his arms he held me.
I looked in his eyes and pulled at his heart strings.
It was in that moment that it dawned on him
that he would fight tooth and nail for me.

The Man of My Life
loves me with love immeasurable.
The Man of My Life
held me with such tender care as if a tiny fragile bird's egg.
The Man of My Life
gave up his heart's desires for mine.

The Man of My Life...
The Man of My life
is one I cannot live without,
is a man like no other
is irreplaceable.
We have built our relationship
on the foundation of memories, both woeful and joyful ones.
He has watched me grow.
He was there when I uttered my first words.
His heart melted at the sound of my voice calling his name for the first time.
He cried tears of joy when I took my first steps.
He felt my pain when I was hurt.
He limps for me when I am injured.
He has proven to me in action what true love is.

The Man of My Life...
The Man of My Life
 Is My Father.

Clementine Tjameya

Never Date Men Like Your Father

Remember when your mother left and your father burned the porridge
so black the house smelled of death for 3 days?
How it hugged the air and stuck to everything you owned?
That you knew something had died?
Remember when your Grandmother had to take you to live with her?
And when you asked if we were coming back and she said soon?
And soon turned into *Kapana*[1] moving from the side of the road to Single Quarters?
And soon turned into 22 years, five months, one day and 55 seconds?

Remember when your Grandmother had to sit in a dimly lit corner of her room at 2 am,
sewing your heart back together again like the last time your parents said they were coming home,
To visit but didn't.
In the end she stopped telling you whenever the birds whispered their visit,
the crickets stopped singing and the night lay still in your heart.
In the end you stop asking.
But in the end, you never stop hoping.
You told yourself they are scared, they were scared they might see each other in you.

Because whenever you cried you saw them holding each other on your face,
like the night they made you.
You see them in the way your face splits into two when you are on the verge of sadness,
one side turning into your father shouting at your mother, the other side leaving.
There will always be an open invitation on your face for sadness,
because your parents have never seen you happy together.
Remember how your father slapped you when you stopped calling him father
and called him by his first name?
Remember the only emotion your father knows well is anger?
He knows how to brew it with no reason.

---

1   Place where street food is sold

Remember your grandmother taught you how to throw a little talcum powder
under your pillow to keep the bad dreams away.
Remember the walks you'd take behind the tall trees.
Remember how she would get on all fours and kiss the earth with her wet lips,
How there was gravel on her mouth
how there was gravel on her teeth.
Remember how she plucked a few sticks
and pounded them?
Remember the day you were returning to the city
when how she pushed the pouch in your hands
and whispered this is how you keep a man darling,
this how you feed on their pity.
Rub this in between your legs at night
and wrap your legs around him.
If you do it right he'll stay.
Remember how you wanted to tell her
you'd never beg a man to stay
even if it was your father.

Veripuami Nandeekua Kangumine

Matutura[1]

I am told by my *kuku*[2],
In this place *katutura*[3]
We are cursed. Plagued by an old lady
Who cried over the grave of her *kuku*,
When they moved her from *ou lokasie*[4].
She wanted her bones exhumed
To preserve an ageless umbilical fibre
Which fosters a rare verve to our Holy Fire.
It was above all, the elixir of their lives,
For god's sake!

As the ancient chains shattered
The old lady lost so much peace
From leaving behind so many pieces.
The rest, she carried in a pelt pouch
Filled with fragments of memories
Coated by a rumbling yester laughter,
One so infectious the old night fell,
Literally.
For the stars and moon had fallen in love
With a people as chilling as morn dew.

---

1   [Place] where we live
2   Granny
3   [Place] where we do not want to live
4   old location

Again, and again, I am told by *kuku*
The old lady now resides in *Oponganda*[5],
Isolated like the twins of *Omatako*[6].
There, in that uninhabitable wilderness
of the Damara Land Petrified Forest
where the breath of God does not howl;
her blemishes find beatific harmony.
As the night globe befits a gleaming halo,
She befits the source of life in Golgotha
Evoking the love out of the *gomchas*[7].

I am told by my *zali*[8],
Who heard it from her father
That our Holy Fire is forever
It turns our hard streets soft as skin,
See how Ana plays at the bus stop.
It evokes the pastors to intercede
A love forgotten, like the Finger of God.
Seaming a new sociospatial device
Curse free, we the young call it 'Tura'
For this is the place where *matutura*.
Protected by an old lady.

Batchotep

---

5   Oponganda Cemetery
6   Twin peaks of the Omatako Mountains
7   Slang for 'criminals'
8   Slang for 'mother'

The *Omaere* That Never Soured

When you don't have a mother
and the lines between childhood and
girlhood begin to blur
you hold onto the first woman you encounter.
A teacher, an aunt, a cousin, a friend.
They teach you how to be an open wound
so as to be accustomed to pain.
And how to handle pain with a straight face.
They teach you how to turn tears into sugar water.
They teach you how to mend a broken heart with gum.
How to hide scars behind beautiful smiles.
And as the world begins to hit you,
They teach you that a girl is like a calabash filled with *omaere*[1],
That all the flies want to contaminate.
These women have wisdom in the headwraps, *doeks*[2] and *otjikaevas*[3].
They, with and without children, will let you call them mother, aunty, ma
They will teach you that in some places you will enter as a child and
leave as a woman, and in other places you enter as a broken woman
and you leave as a god.

Veripuami Nandeekua Kangumine

---

1 Otjiherero for sour milk
2 Afrikaans for head scarf
3 Otjiherero for headdress

Namibian Beauty

Eyes as dazzling as diamonds
Hair as vibrant as the Mopane tree
Skin as smooth as Sossusvlei sand dunes

Mind as profound as the Fish River Canyon
Character as sophisticated as the Twyfelfontein
Determination as enduring as the Skeleton Coast

Born from the soil of her ancestors, her spirit is free
Onandjokwe to Windhoek, village to city life
Adventurous and brave, all the world is hers to explore

Beauty Ndapanda

Lid smile

Her smile
Lids all
She passes
Rare breed
Leads the breeze

Her walk
Leaves them back
And begging
Swing of her hips
Mutes them all

Her posh smile
Brings cold chills
Down throats
Her smell
Has them melt

Way she talks
Has her followed
Way she leans
Leaves them captured

Her voice
Eases the surrounds
Her eyes
Stroke the ground
Her beauty
Leaves them
Still and shaken

She slides
In no haste
Her perfume
So serene
Her taste
So sincere
Activating cells

Her shine
Her gait
Way she leans
Tells a story

Her beauty
Arrests a bunch
Her presence
Violates lunch

Her walk
Her talk
Is all they remember

Lid smile

Magnus Elius Tjiueza

Hail to the Queen

Women like me climb summits, defy step and seed.
You see
Women like me are born with sword in hand
Word that births fruitful planes and plans.
My womb secretes a crimson ointment to anoint my wounds.
We came to heal
Eight generations of misappropriated and
Displaced power
Poverty and defeat.
Women like me write poetry for all the women hidden in me
Reconciling miracles to ourselves
Raptured
Flawed and still standing tall
We sing through war
Bayete!!
Hail to the queen.

Zemha Gawachas

I am We

Under the Namib sun a boy looked at me,
A boy desired me,
A boy spoke to me,
A boy questioned me,
A boy listened to me,
A boy searched me,
And I said: "Boy, find man."

The boy searched himself,
The boy saw himself,
The boy planted himself,
The boy watered himself,
The boy grew,
The boy became man.

I saw man,
I let man touch me, gently
I let man in,
I opened up and let man penetrate my deepest thoughts, my deepest fears.

Man spilled his seed of wisdom into my sea of nurture,
Man died, Woman died,
Man and I became one,
I am not she and man is not he,
I AM WE.

Jane Mungabwa

John Muafangejo's prayer[1]

Hear me, oh God.

You know
I was
but a simple Kwanjama,
a Namibian man
with base needs
I did not understand
and a love
I could not hide.

When
you touched me,
I was left
troubled.
Misunderstood,
I cut into lino
and by reduction
told my truth,
printing jet black areas
within white borders
for all to see.

---

1 John Muafangejo (1943 – 1987), Namibian artist who became internationally known for his linocuts

Ah,
I learned
the ways of my people
and was told
it was black.
I discovered
the ways of white people
and it was
shades of night.

So,
through my fingertips
you guided me
to create this body,
born
from my soul,
that grew legs
to stride
over boundaries
I could not understand
and I now
have left behind.

Please let my brothers and sisters,
see my work
as my communion
with them.
I bring them the pure gold that never rusts.

This
is my life.
Let them slice it into
kapana,
Eat
let my black ink
flow for them.
Drink.

Oh Lord.
you know my prayers
for peace
in this land.
I did not understand.

Please
Christ
let my body
be transparent,
and a light,
for all to see.

Jesus,
let my brothers
not scavenge over my
dead bones,
the shackles,
I left behind.

Forgive
their vulgar ways,
as your priests
absolved mine.
you tolerated my rage
I did not know why.

God.
You know me
You know all cultures.
all whys,
all mysteries
and wishes.
My compatriots
I left behind
do not understand
how I now,
One with you,
can understand
the darkness
of the tortured soul
I left behind.
Amen.

Pedro Vorster

Alike

You watch them

Their clumsy portrayal, their distort ways.

You look, and paint your own picture

Of them

As if you were a mere spectator of their species.

What if they look at you the same way?

Judging, wondering why or why not…questioning your choices, your being, your reputation.

How sure are you your name doesn't sound the same?

Mere, simple…bringing no apostrophe, smile nor emoji to memory – plain, common. Ordinary.

If what makes you you, and what makes them them were swapped…would we all not still be under one umbrella?

Children, faulty, simple…Human.

Remaliah Margarida Chingufo

Crystalize

If we are the salt of the Earth
Let these truths crystalize on your ear lobes
For on the periodic table of elements we are Xn
Meaning Christian
That is double covalent properties, belief in the prophecies
Of triple 9
Of microchips
Of blue pill blues while living in the matrix
That is your android paranormal paranoia
Your phone tethered to your wrist and the code streams embedded under your skin
To serve the locomotive motion of your heart's desire

Freeman Ngulu

Surface Tension arises from the polar nature of the water molecule

At an artificial water-hole, where benches
set back from a barbed fence protect
us, or them baby, we
see hippos. Hippos! on the bank.
Big, broad backs, solid, mat. And miles
from where they might belong.
But we're busy. Unpacking, pouring gin,
berating the fool who forgot
the tonic then kissing
to make up when it's been there in that pocket
all along. The land up there,
past Okahandja, is so flat. Cleared of people,
the empty stretches for miles
in every direction and when we turn, cold glasses
pressed to sweaty temples
and they're gone, we see nothing
but tiny shrubs and the sky in the still pond.
Not one hippo left.
What kind of family collectively hallucinates hippos? And what
makes them forget
that space where giants wait just under the surface.

Tessa Harris

Authenticity

African cab driver
Weaves through spaces like liquid gold
Wholly illegal moving, no seat belts working
Loud music all the windows are down
Sweating out summer in worn seats
Pinkie nail on his right finger long and yellowing
Perhaps in another life he is a mob boss
Dressed like he is on a perpetual holiday
Knows all the short cuts, assures you
Today you are one of his many cousins
One hand driving series, multi task genius
Texts from his girlfriend who needs a ride to university
Bobbing and weaving from a to b, with a lax urgency
Cheeky grin in rear view mirror when his wife calls
When angry drivers hoot, he hoots right back
Like Sunday service greetings
You are never a stranger on these roads
You are a late opportunity, unpaid school fees
Outraged when pulled over, don't they know
These roads that are not ours
They belong to African cab drivers
African cab drivers and their glory

Kina Indongo

WHAT'S WRONG?

What's wrong?

What's wrong with having girl children
One after the other, with no son in sight or at last?
What's wrong with a woman doing it herself
With no ring or heir?
What's wrong with being a career driven woman
With little or no time for nonsense or man?
What's wrong with a woman
Who packs her bags and belongings before it's too late?
If there is somebody who is wrong it is you and the like-minded!

Saara Kadhikwa

Stir Not My Dear One

Darkness summons doom
Sadness befalls and overwhelms a being
And sunken a dear loving heart.
Hear it pound heavily against the chest
Listen! To this sound, a sound of fear
For a dear one is soon to come from the dark path,
where liquor has ballooned his belly.

Watch him sway left, right and centre
Hear him utter unintelligible words
which manifest into phrases filled with insults,
Insults that spur out in arrows
Arrows that barrel into my delicate heart
Ow dear! I am an African woman.

My dear one sluggishly walks to our room.
My dear children dash for shelter
Look at my dear one! There he stands as if dancing, as if shivering.
His eyes seem to bulge out of his skull
As though a mouse has been accidently trapped by his beer crate
My eyes fall on his unzipped slacks
His mouth opens and in slow murmur, demands for food.

Within, questions flock like missiles, but I dare not ask
For that heavy hand, many a time thudded my body
The heavy hand that I have fed,
The heavy hand that holds other village women
Ow dear! I am an African woman.

My dear one sits to eat.
His tongue frogs out like a serpent meeting its prey.
I sit and watch him eat, until he has had his fill.
In ten or five seconds, he dozes off
His snores can be heard by neighbouring villages
But yet we soundly sleep and wake by the break of dawn
To toil the fields and sing off our pains and burdens
While the rain cools our hearts and the birds soothe our souls as they flock by.

My dear one wakes to kill his hangover.
Watch him go, that's my dear one
My truly "for better, for worse".

Anneli Nghikembua

You Broke Me, Daddy

I'm cold
I'm freezing cold
Don't say I never said, because I always told;
And no matter when the story will be spoken of, it's still old.

Come and see daddy, come and see the monster that you with your cold demeanour mould.
Couldn't you see that instead of hard blows, mama's cries and booze, all I needed was a
daddy to hold?

I sought your affection in the beds and arms of men and women who are cold like you,
And no matter how much pain they caused me, I stayed; I had to be brave because I felt
that by trying to save them in a way I was saving you daddy.

You never even noticed how much I cried, but then again, maybe you noticed daddy but
you just never cared to be my dad, you never tried.

All I needed was your love daddy, but all you gave me was rage.
But it's okay now daddy, it's okay.
I won't cry anymore daddy,
I hope you're proud now daddy,
'cause I'm cold just like you.

Jane Mungabwa

Anomaly

I have a fierceness that is both proud and lonely,
A tearing, a howling,
A hunger and thirst.
A strength that would die fighting,
Kicking,
Screaming,
That wouldn't stop until the last breath had been wrung from its body.
The will to take one's place in the world.
To say "I am". To say "I am".

Valery Mkabeta

Domestic worker[1]

Work, work, work,
Always on the job
Up at four,
Outside I go

Make the *vetkoek*, fry the fish, the *oshikundu* is ready…

It's six o' clock,
Time to freshen up in my room… too many drunks in the neighbourhood
who target women
So my bucket, face cloth and my room do the trick just fine.

My uniform slithers onto my skin as a python swallowing its prey
It notifies the whole world that I am a domestic worker.
And yet I know that,
I am that little fairy that just kissed your cheek,
that person who will bring you joy in my own ways.

I am not just a domestic but for now I will cover up my beautiful being with this Uniform.
Shoes, Jersey, Umbrella but something is missing… of course, my handbag…
oh and my *vetkoek* and fish for breakfast.
I shall enjoy this on the long bus ride to the other side of town.
Luckily the bus stop is not that far.
Six thirty on the dot.

I never miss the bus, the stop is only four shacks away.
My seat is cold and waiting for me to heat it up.
So now let's see…
Napkin, and *vetkoek* with fish… two of each…

---

1   The poem 'I, Domestic Worker' by Herman H. Le Roux was posted on Facebook on 8 January
    2020, a year after this contribution was received

The taxis are the owners of the roads, no respect for anything dead or alive.
What kind of a society are these cities breeding?
No respect for the elders, for people,
racism here, sexism there …
What are we really doing?

The bus ride is an hour long.
Thoughts, thoughts, are stuck in my head but where do I start?

Five years have passed and I am still where I started.
The anguish in my belly, the thoughts in my head.
Never ending story,
Is this what they call adulthood?
Is this what they call city life?
Is this what they call living?

A slave to the machine is what I have become…
Wake up, clean someone's house then come home…
Cook for eight people, phone my children then go to sleep…
The same routine for the past five years!

What would they do without me?
Where is the justice and pride in earning ninety Namibia Dollars a day?

Ina-Maria Shikongo

The man with the cap

Who is the man with the cap?
His story about where he's been keeps changing
But he can name all his mental illnesses and their treatments
It's not what you know that counts; it's what you say
He is the man with the cap

Who is the man with the cap?
My story about where I'm from keeps changing
But I can name all the employers who gave me my mental ailments
It's not what you know but who, in this corrupted world
I am the man with the cap

Who is the man with the cap?
He's the man you don't want to see
Whose ancestors were survivors of genocide and parents victims of colonialism
Their blood waters his freedom, and mine
He is the man with the cap

Who is the man with the cap?
The sought-after man, the man-about-town
Whose ancestors made a killing in Africa and whose parents worked for the Church
Amazing grace! How sweet the sound…
I am the man with the cap

Who is the man with the cap?
He's not looking for trouble, boss, he just wants to say something
Like all of us, he's trying to tell you a story, hoping you'll spare him a coin
It's an ill wind that blows nobody good
He is the man with the cap

Who is the man with the cap?
I just want to get home, as we all do
And not have to deal any more with these privileged white men, nor this parasitic black elite
If the cap fits, wear it
I am the man with the cap

Who is the man with the cap?
Who holds dominion over this vast planet? And who are any of us
On this pale blue dot, Spaceship Earth? If you try to define our madness,
Then you surely must be mad
We are the men with the cap

Hugh Ellis

Dordabis

An hour's drive from the capital
Surrounded by virginal woodlands and fenced pristine farms
Lies a tiny settlement with an equally tiny post office
A health clinic and police station
A primary school all squeezed like the proverbial tinned sardines.

Yet vast lands surround the private farms
Sandwiching the misery evident to the newcomer
Of a community riddled with alcoholism
Prematurely aged faces well beyond their years
Unmasking the discontent and disappointment,
Of an indifferent Christmas day.

Amidst the well-manicured farmhouses,
Absentee Landlords, valuable wildlife,
Trophy hunters from distant lands in pursuit of pleasure
In air-conditioned 4x4s and D4Ds
In their booked guest lodges and farm houses
Attract curious glares from the downtrodden.

An image of my Christmas from the bustling distractions of city and family
First in awe of the beautiful environment
But left with tortured memories
Of the wretched conditions and the cloud
Of poverty, despair and desperation
Screaming loud from what the eyes could see;
Bewildering how this could be and wither the spirit of ubuntu?

Is this the land of the brave or the faint hearted?
A disgruntled majority, landless and waterless
Hopelessness galore amidst gluttonous feasts
Where many consume in festive indulgence
Others sad, hungry and angry
Igniting my literal juices compensating the guiltiness
I am not responsible for.

The constant begging for cigarettes
Nicotine slaves forgetting bread
A moral dilemma on that hot Christmas day
Remaining etched on my conscience.
Corrugated iron shacks, others decorated for the day
A veneer of normalcy in the hardscrabble rural existence
Unable to hide the smell of squalor and neglect.
This ramshackle existence beggars belief
The Namibian house[1], hijacked or looted by the not so needy?
Or the greedy, leaving the destitute poorer and forgotten.
The sight of conspicuous consumption
Of the sumptuous feasts and decent outfits openly enjoyed
Expensive whiskies dampened by Dordabis
Disheartened the festive spirit but inspired this verse
Immortalizing the desperation of Dordabis through the ink that flowed
Not a Christmas like that again!

Charles Mlambo

---

1   President Hage Geingob used the metaphor of a house under construction in a State
    of the Nation address (2015) to stress the need to include all Namibians in the project
    of nation-building

Shshsh...listen...

Shshsh...listen...
The ground sizzles in the heat
The mirage of the horizon hazy with dust
They're coming...
You can hear their hooves crunching through the dry delicate veld
Their call echoes across the land
Their stench rises as they near the soiled pan
Slurping and sucking from the cesspool, once a watering hole for all
Laden and bellowing they scour the area for signs of fresh green growth
Ripping, crushing, destroying relentlessly
Leaving no trace of endemic life behind

Shshsh... listen...
A baby cries, stomach aching, cramping
Eyes squinted from the constant pestering of flies
Water, the life vein, is contaminated
Sickness prevails where young and old are first to undeservedly suffer
Mothers are out searching, with well-trained eyes they scan the bush
The traces of veld food trampled and destroyed
Aia[1] must move deeper into Nyae Nyae
Leaving behind the sick and weak in search of nourishment and medicine

---

1   Mother

Tamah[2]
Dcaa[3]
Dchun[4]
G!xoa[5]
Tci-||a'asi[6]
Toq[7]
‡'Om-n|aisi[8]
||Xamtci||oq'oro[9]

Aia, mama, !ui!ui, da'abi!oa[10]
A successful forage, but each time further and further afield
We are worried about those we love, back at the *n!ore*[11]
Now, so much further away than before
We begin the long journey home

Shshsh…listen…
Chief Tsamkxao ‡Oma shakes his head and rubs his bare feet over the earth
They are coming…
They have been coming for many years now
We have kept them back
Fighting for the protection of our land
Kieviet, he was fighting with me
We were young, strong during the *n!ai*[12]
We shot those *gumi*[13] if they came across the border

---

2   Tsamma melon
3   Gemsbok cucumber
4   Bush potato
5   Water-root kambroo
6   Seeds
7   Brown honey
8   Baobab fruit
9   Devil's claw
10 Mother, grandmother, older sister, children
11 village
12 war
13 cattle

But now we are old
The *gumi* are too many
And we've turned to paper for protection
We write and write
We meet and meet
Zero action from local police
Our people, the *Ju|'hoansi*, are sick and suffering
Kashipembe[14] riding in on hooves
Eroding our bodies and minds
Feeding addiction
Breaking and scattering families
We are poisoned
As unlawful invaders continue to move in
Depleting unforgivingly
Our carefully protected resources
This needs to stop
Now

Shshsh...listen....
The cattle are coming!

Kerry Jones

---

14 Home-brewed drink with addictive chemicals added

Syringes

Dr Prescriptions
Piercing, searing syringes
I wonder
Am I sustaining my sickness?
Or my health?
Agonizing injections
Dr Urges
The stings will regenerate
Your cells

Kavevangua Kahengua

THE weak-end OF THE WEEK

Monday

Is mourn-day
The silent CRY of a body in pain
You got flu
And you are feeling blue

TUESDAY

You choose to tie your shoes
And solve the issues
But your feet aren't fit
To stand the day

WEDNESDAY

Is wOrse-day
Where in this land is the land to land
And descend upon a life that's yours
The question is answered by a yawn
And words fall back in line
At the command of…
"You must work hard and pay the rent!!"

THURSDAY

Is thoughts-day
When the mind is blind
The eyes cannot see
The road from Home to Work
Should have a name change
From Independence Avenue
To Indebt-payment Avenue

FRIDAY

Free the slave, and get the money
Alcohol says "I'll-call-you-all"
And you shall answer
Tonight, the dance floor is the death flow
Of a people zombified by the scripted reality

SATURDAY

You sit-a-day
Satisfied
Unsatisfied
And the glass is re-filled
And the label reads:
'Half-empty-Half-zombie'

SUNDAY

The sun is out to howl-a-lie!
God is a European male…
Who created the female as an afterthought
And whoever believes the lie shall have a terminal life
Interrupted by tithes and offerings to an Amen that ain't so
An end that doesn't end and a full stop that doesn't stop the fool!

Prince Kamaazengi Marenga

Apartheid

Chained, oppression anchored
The world beckons
But his pen encounters writer's block
As the ink tries to dance away
24 years of the system of segregation.
He writes with intent to nail the
Bloodshed under colonialism to peace
And serenity.
Deprived of liberty, his peace and
Serenity sent into exile
His freedom is a threat, so is his
Existence.
The moon bleeds and his nights are long
He is haunted with the homeless breath
Of his forefathers.
His master is a monster who resembles
The harshness of a whip that burns and
Leaves its mark like heat on a light
Skinned person in cruel summer.
Days are short but his spirit is not, even
With no external help to offer solace, he
Fights for his peace and not only for
Honours

And through the gun fire and riots like
The state of the country at the death of
Swapo activist Lubowski, he achieves
Freedom from oppression and gains the
State of being free.
The homeless breath of his ancestors
Becomes a doctrine of peace and freedom.
He comes from a lineage of survivors
And he is reminded, every time he is tempted
To lose his ways and love for his country
A broken heart bleeds red.
So did the country in its fight for independence
And with a strong will and desire for
Nationalism he has made it, so he signs
Off;
March 21, 1990
But he is older than time, more than 20
Years later, he's still trying to dance away
The years of oppression.

Nandu Ndabeni

Struggle Kid*

Frieda wanted change and her story to be told
Now her bullet-pierced body lies in the streets lifeless and cold
The bright sun of today was supposed to sink slowly into the promised hills of gold.
Frieda was born into the liberation struggle some hero's daughter
"Your parents' sacrifice was not in vain," is what our leaders taught her
Now the same leaders are responsible for her innocent slaughter.

Shocking to learn, through police brutality Frieda died
Our Namibian constitution clearly states Life is a given Right
And that the government shall protect every Namibian's life.

Fighting to survive is all that Frieda ever knew
Remember even the liberation struggle was started by a few
"They're killing my people, Mr President what will you do?"

Frieda wanted change and her story to be told
Now her bullet-pierced body lies in the streets lifeless and cold
The bright sun of today was supposed to sink slowly into the promised hills of gold.

*For Frieda Ndatipo, a victim of police brutality

Onesmus Shimwafeni

Land of broken dreams

A land of broken dreams,
is that where I'll end up too?

A migration to greener pastures,
Only to be greeted by tin pastures.

To become a rich man's puppet is the equation.
A cry that is heard but not noticed.

A hunter-gatherer's life was better.
Civilized only to suffer.

A land of broken dreams,
Where hope is forgotten it seems.

Engelhardt Unaeb

Trouble in paradise

'Namibia, land of the brave'
A liberated, chainless slave,
Who digs her own grave
With deeds as cold as ice.

Security, a basic need,
Has been encroached on by a weed
Of a foolish, heartless breed.
Our liberty now wears a price.

As dunes to deserts are we to crime,
With misled minds as an enzyme
Which speeds the destruction of our prime.
Nevertheless, we will see them diced.

My words are of great cause:
Until we unite against the outlaws,
We will be at the mercy of their claws
And our savannah will be no paradise.

Hijenduanao Uanivi

FIGHTING
THE STORM
WITHIN

Fighting the Storm Within

For me it's not like drowning, and it's not sudden; it's like light rain.

It starts with feeling like you bother the people you confide in
or that no one really understands or cares what you're going through.

So you stop confiding.
Then your relationships with other people lack depth
because you no longer share the deepest parts of yourself,
so you worry that your friendships and relationships are superficial.

Then you worry that you're being superficial.
So you work really hard on being happy,
and grateful,
and kind,
and everything that is the opposite of what you're afraid you'll become;
of what you have become.

For me it's not like drowning, it's like light rain.

It's not really bothersome at first
but the longer you're in it, the worse you feel.

That light pitter-patter on your skin begins to feel like pins and needles.
The more it rains the harder it is to see clearly
the more saturated your clothes become,
the more weighed down you feel,
the less you notice about your surroundings.
It is only the rain that you see, feel, taste, hear, and smell.
You're constantly irritated from it so your patience is thin and you're just one tap away
from becoming a storm.

For me it's not like drowning, it's like light rain.

And everyone keeps telling you to just get out of the rain then,
not realising that it rains wherever you go.

Gloria Ndilula

Depression

My name is melancholy
Alias depression.
Mental disorder.
Psych-
Is my family name.
Many hear of me
Yet few fully comprehend me.
I'm only here
for these three:
To steal your joy, peace & happiness
Your aspirations, dreams & hopes.
To deprive you of sleep
Appetite & zeal.
To bombard you
With despair, exhaustion, recklessness
Fears, worries, agitation
Numbness, suicide.
Remember
I multiply and triumph
But can also be
Fought and defeated
Depending on your approach.
Either you join me
In shackles, in bondage
At psychiatry, at Malkamp
In cemetery, in hell
Or beat me
Through acknowledgement & acceptance
Through prayer & positivity
By talk therapy or treatment.

Saara Kadhikwa

He cries in silence

I know you hurt
I know you cry
I know you wish you could lay your head on your mother's lap
And hear her whisper "it will be alright."
But you dare not
It's taboo.

I know you hurt
I know you cry
I know you wish you could tell her exactly what she did to upset you
And relieve yourself from the anger boiling inside you.
But you dare not
It's taboo.

I know you hurt
I know you cry
I know you wish you could tell someone what happened that night.
But you dare not
It's taboo.
Tears are a man's taboo.

Mercy George

Heart of Stone

Heart of stone,
Envious and so alone.
Angry in tone,
Refusing to condone,
The desire for a broken bone.

Heart of stone.
Envious of my throne,
And wanting me thrown.
Refusing to atone,
To having not known.

Lazarus Shatipamba

Raining without water

It can't rain all the time
Then why is it still raining?
It's raining but it's not wet
I'm crying but I'm not sad yet
I'm running to stand still
Meek as a lamb with an iron will
I can't remember but I can't forget
I give everything, yet everything I get
I'm deaf to the world, still I can hear you speak
I'm forever hiding but still I seek
I feel quite depressed, but I'm just fine
The clock is ticking, but we're out of time
I'm not even considering, and yet I might
It's raining without a cloud in sight.

Dalene Gous

He

Like a thief drawn into night
Like a storm in the midst of time
He creeps slowly to steal light
Drowning by waves of his water, all that's sublime

Like a painted creation
Like a force of swirling wind
He stalks, not a blink hesitation
Scattering mercy moments of happy from mind

Like torment of water still as glass
Like tame sheep that wolf thoughts sing
He devours all within, not a leftover to pass
Flowing with hunger, lust to you bring

Like a patient lion waiting for prey
Like a poisonous flower, pretty as can be
He pounces, strangling life within each day
Blinds and deceives, delirious to see

Like the sweet call of a siren conjuring death
Like a strike of lightning without thunder
He looms until close to remove your last breath
Depression the spell you're under

Christelize Elleen Meintjies

Hush

Sundays are rough for people like me.
A vicious heretic, that's me.
I've spent most my nights and conversations scrutinizing the religion I've
been served.
I've left my friends and family stunned.
Upset and shook.
They say it's blasphemous to call the Bible "just a book"
So I've toned it down, to "if that's what you believe" looks.

See I'm no atheist.
I believe that a God exists.
But I have questions,
I page from Genesis to Revelations,
And I seek to have open and real conversations,
But I get turned down, as if asking if God really loves all people when he
slaughtered numerous tribes, is a sin worthy of getting stoned.

I am the woman at the well.
Jesus' grace saved me from getting murdered but all is not well
I have to live my life in a shell.
Hiding from the people who've heard my words,
And still condemn me with their stares.
I am... the condemned.

Every day, I pray for forgiveness for being inquisitive.
Every Sunday, I sacrifice myself as a lamb for my sins of questioning.
And I suppress, and I suppress.
And I dress
Myself down to fit into the perceived godly perceptions.
I am unhappy, but I die at the rejection.

Esther Nantana

Concrete Cold

Concrete cold
Keeps me safe
Captured in my thoughts
Uncomfortable, saving face
Limits my flow
Slowly slowly
Concrete cold

Concrete cold
Holds my heart
Jailed in comfort
Restless
Broken in shards
Softly shattering
Softly softly
Concrete cold

Concrete cold
Divides desire
Locked up in hours
Dampening my soul
Diminished
A blank slate
Erased erased
Concrete cold

Sanmari Steenkamp

Disconnect

I see, I hear, I feel
Words, people, things
Once in line
It was mine

I see, I hear, I feel
Things, people, places
Now distant concepts
Like brick to water

Reaching back
I see my selves
One here
One there
Once here
Now there

Lost

Sanmari Steenkamp

The cliff beneath your feet

Nihility, the lack of daily order
The cliff forever beneath your feet
Unbalanced, these feet
Hope nowhere in sight
Reason, preoccupied
"Jump" they tell you
Where are your friends?
Who brought you here?
To the cliff beneath your feet

Where are your friends?
Go to them
You
You are your friends

Interrupt reason
Tell her you need to talk
Hope is hiding in plain sight
On the other side of the cliff
Care is waiting to walk you all home safely

Aquila Bartholomeus

Somewhere

Somewhere
there are minke whales singing hymns in my belly
Lonely cries beneath my star-lined ribs
Somewhere
there's a seafoam & driftwood lapping against my skin
Drowning me in vertiver notes.
Somewhere
the winds crack & cry through my hollow frame.
The rains come & the tides swell and my throat is all sand and gravel
And your name is stuck against my tongue, beating against the backs of my teeth.
Somewhere
A whistle cries & the lighthouse fades and I am floating in the inkbled sky.
Somewhere
I'm slightly losing myself, my last breath is leaving my body
And I
Don't feel a thing.

Omaano Itana

NOT BY HEART
BUT BY FISTS

The Beat of Samantha

Samantha, Samantha!
Drunk he calleth her name.
Up the stairs he cometh,
My food, my food, he shouts!

Her frightened stare into darkness,
Groweth her pupil!
Pupils of black marble alike.
At the borders of her sight,
Behold her heart's keeper, the beater!

Fight & flight, but right deprived.
Cries for help, utters no sound!

Bad words, mad words, she listens.
Fear, fear for fists of thunder!
Eyes beaten blue just as violets,
Why all the violence?

Red wrists, instead of roses!
Is violence the new romance?
Oh my, that's the beat of Samantha!
Not by heart, but by fists!

Simson Mario Ochurub

Dear Perpetrator

Broken glass

Shattered dreams

Tainted soul

I was only 10 years old when your archaeological tool examined the evidence in my temple

Why?

Why did you take advantage of my excitement when your taxi dropped by that day?

You told me you wanted to shower me with sweets

And I fell for something sweet, instead of realising that the sour would overpower

my life

But I should have known

You drove rather quickly

I asked you to stop

Take me home

I begged, but all you did was suffocate the words in my throat with your sweaty palms

Forcefully caging me

I tried calling Mama and Papa

Hoping that they could remove the shackles you chained me with

But all I felt was fear wrapping its arms around me

Loudly calling me home

I thought you were my friend

But you lied

You lied

You disembodied the frame it took me 10 years, 4 months and 2 weeks to build

Declaring victory over a body I can no longer call my own

The shreds of blood didn't seem to make you quit

You kept coming at me

Not only did you hurt the parts that made me a little girl

You felt the need to steal them when you broke down my wall into tiny bricks

Exposing different parts of me to your friends

Selling each and every one of them a piece

While leaving my insides for those that have taken care of me

I didn't know that when I joined you in the taxi that day, it would be my last

You broke me

Shattered me

Demolished me

Leaving my insides for the hounding dogs to shred and further diminish

I regret mistaking your smile for kindness

I wish I had stayed home

I wish I had given myself the opportunity to shower my parents with love

To academically grow and fulfil my dream of becoming a teacher

To cradle my little babies in my arms, while marrying the one man my father taught me about

But now, I will never get that chance

You stole my life because money was way more important than the growth of a little girl

You didn't even have the decency to give me a proper funeral

Parts of my being lay in a heavy coffin, not enough to orchestrate the music of a complete human

And now, I am left singing to the tunes of the angels

While you run away from being chained to your sins

Broken glass

Shattered dreams

Tainted soul

From

A 10 year old girl who could have been[1]

Tulipomwene Kalunduka

---

1   Cheryl Avihe Ujaha, mutilated and murdered 28 August 2018

My dear Maria

She was only sixteen,
when she appeared within
his predatory sights.
Her appearance brightened his eyes like city lights.
With stealth he got close to her,
a young blooming flower,
her eyes sparkling with curiosity and innocence.
He sensed her materialistic wishes with his experience.

Her acquaintance he made
for her luxuries he paid,
his trap was laid.

Blinded by infatuation,
she showered him with affection.
Never did she refuse him permission.

He entered her eden,
made a path well trodden.

She was in bliss
so she missed the hiss,
that came every time
she went left, when he wanted her right.
Never did she feel his hug or grip on her hand too tight.
Ahhh, my dear Maria, once so beautiful, alive and brave
Now I only see you when I go to the grave.
Ah, my dear Maria...

Aristides 'Are' Sambiliye

Drug Addict

To impress my peers I took one puff
After that puff, there was no way out
Dropped out of school to feed my addiction
Mandrax and hubbly a shoulder to lean on

Every Friday a party day
Party freaks crowded where we stayed
Now that I walk next to my shoes
Nobody wants to walk next to me

My bright smile faded away
Drug abuse discoloured my teeth
My fingertips are as hard as stone
My face is full of stretch marks

I had to cover them with tattoos
At such a young age, I had wrinkles
At home am innocent as a saint
In the streets, even dogs hesitate to bark.

Alex Swartbooi

Violence

You knew, didn't you?
You felt that train leave you,
in the dead of the night terror arrives
All your worth in a small bag

This is how storms are made
When he shuts doors to the conversations
When his body says there has been another
Uses force to break all your locks
browsing through without meaning to stay
Lumbers up your stairs, real loud
you hear the floor boards moaning
Like bloodied nose, like that time you tried to defend yourself
How he shoves you out your own body
and turns you into a riot

Three thousand village women
Blooming in your chest,
arms and legs lead heavy with bruising
Wailing mothers with missing daughters
As you too become another memorial of tragedy

There are not many sirens in your country,
Blessings, or perhaps
the women in this country prefer to die in silence

Kina Indongo

Who's More Violent?

We speak of gender based violence which remains biased towards women.
We forget the nanny who burned a toddler with boiled water.
Who's more violent?

The man who cuts out his heart and throws it away
Or the woman whose heart resembles the artic, cold and frozen?
Who's more violent?

He who rapes and strangles a toddler until the life drains from it
Or she who mistreats her husband's bastard offspring?
Who's more violent?

The man who cat-calls women walking by
Or the woman who falsely accuses men of rape?
Who's more violent?

The sugar daddy extorting young girls for quick pleasures
Or the bitter baby mama who lies about child support?
Who's more violent?

If men are trash what does that say about the women who love them?
If women are bitches what does that say about the men who marry them?
Who's more violent?

Men are brutal, sadistic, cold blooded killers.
Women are cunning, deceitful, liars, cold blooded assassins.
So answer me this, Who's more violent?

Marco Kalunduka

SHADOWS
OF THE
UNKNOWN

Darkness

In darkness, she lost herself
covered in a blanket of night,
blackened was her reality.

Shadows of the unknown
lurked about.
She feared darkness within,
darkness itself.

A cold rope
Its grip she felt,
sapping the life out of her.

Frozen, soaked in angst,
she glared at darkness.
Shadows bearing witness,
knowing yet distant.

Darkness swallowed her whole.
There she was, staring at her sorrow
dangling above.
Her pain used to have a shrine
within her lifeless body.

Like a leaf swinging
gently dropping,
kissing the dirt
Then burrowing deeper,
into the crevices of the earth.
In darkness she lost herself.

Tuli Phoenix

Death, be my friend

Where are you? Do you know me?
I am your biggest fan – you haunt my every dream
So take my hand and walk with me.

Your perfect totality comforts me
It's reassuring … there's no turning back
You're smooth and omnipresent
None should evade your looming presence!

While others fear you, try to elude your doom
My every vein and limb
Desire your complete invasion
Oblivious to your brutal definiteness, captivated by your mystery.

Death, will you walk with me?

Bronwen A Beukes

What a perfect day to die

Sky swimming with white-grey
Birds singing sweetly
Cool kiss of dew drops
Warm glow of your smile
What a perfect day to die

Light showers of rain drops
Fresh smell of wet dirt
Bloom of flowers
Blossoms of your eyes
What a perfect day to die

Caress of sweet condensed wind
Rivers flowing from rain
Rustle of leaves in the trees
Whispering softly your name
What a perfect day to die

Christelize Elleen Meintjies

This isn't a poem

It's an apology for all the times I lobbed, left hooks in my spine and left hooks anchored
Still stuck in your skin in high hopes that I'll never lose hold of you again.
This is me previously convincing myself never to skydive again,
Being that your parachute only came through after I had hit rock bottom.
This is me sitting in a half-filled bathtub, picking the daggers from beneath the folds of my skin.
Do you know how much blood a human can lose before they pass on or pass away?
When the paramedics find me, they'll say it was sudden cardiac arrest.
You'll know it was because I kept a live grenade in my chest for a heart.
But I've been taking my time digesting your absence.
I've never yearned for resurrection the way I did when I walked in to your dangling feet after
having taken one too many chill pills.
So now I just sit here with ears echoing forever for ever and a throat itching with unsaid
emotions.
Looking back I understand why you took your life.
And as crude as this sounds, I wish you'd done so quietly, without leaving your noose around
my neck or your footprints across my heart, but I guess slitting wrists isn't that hard when you
wear your heart on your sleeves.
Please just accept this as my apology
The one I'm still pulling from between my teeth.
I know you made me promise not to miss you too much.
It was never my intention to lie at the feet of your tombstone, bleeding, trying to cough up our
memories.

Omaano Itana

Escape from civilized life

For Etienne my identical twin (15.01.1949–02.03.2012)
Infinitely gentle, infinitely suffering brother
Your final withdrawal into the rock cathedral
of the Erongo wilderness, your flight from pain,
Where you ceded your physical beauty,
Your final escape from the fallibility of civilized life
After T.S. Elliot

André du Pisani

Dear Little Soul within My Soul

Sustenance was never my yearning
But I endeavoured to make peace with it
Because of you.

Weeping was never my comfort
But I lay awake all night
Because of you.

My mind incessantly racing during nights on end
My pillow soaked wet with whimpering tears
Until it can absorb no more
Until my tears overflow
Until my habitation becomes
Nothing More
than an ocean of tears,
an ocean of tears
In which I drown.

Whether I developed gills or not
I am not certain
But I found that I could breathe better in this ocean
I found a sense of calming peace
In this melancholic ocean
Although it is my flesh that is cut
It is my spirit that suffers the affliction of my flesh.

I could feel your rage as you forced your exit
Your rage caused me such pain.
Your rage caused me such numbing pain.

And now...

And now I am part of the orchestra in this convalescent home
And all I see is crimson
I might not have seen your dwelling place collapse
But I felt it collapse
And by the time I realised
It was reduced to nothing but crimson
Your body left mine
And it was all in crimson
Your heart became nothing but crimson
Your eyes…
Your limbs…
All crimson.

Child, dear child
What your affliction was
I do not know
What ailed you
I do not know
But one thing that I know for certain
Is that your pain was beyond measure
Is that your pain was unbearable
Because I felt it with you
I felt it with you from the start.

Such was the relationship we had
Two separate beings
Two separate hearts
Two separate souls
That shared the same blood
That shared one body
one weary body
And we knew that sooner or later
One of us had to leave

I am overwhelmed by the thought
That you are reduced to crimson
But I find solace in the thought
Of you being free from affliction
Dear little beating heart
Dear little soul within my soul

Clementine Tjameya

Tribute to a survivor

Cancer
Silently you sneak into that which was not yours,
Robbed me of peace and being,
I was all woman and beautiful
Till you came to test my worth.
I broke down
I cried
Was less of me
Filled with pain
You took all that defined me
Left me naked and half
Filled with anger and pain
I sat in mud wondering
Looking up
To see a different path
I rise to fight
Slowly to rediscover self and worth
It was not your place to be
I overcame pain through faith
Strengthened by support
I looked you in the eye
And started laughing because
I was greater than you
My strides became stronger
As I walked away from your clutches
Once I lost nearly
I turn back
I took back
Never to be robbed again
I smile
I live
Because it's greater than you Cancer
For I am human
I am to live and love
I am to be healthy and happy

Martha Sibila |Khoëses

The pursuit of happiness

There is a ghost that follows my trail,
its stare in my back has made me frail.
I turn around and wave my hand,
just to watch it claim my steps in the sand.
Standing my ground I utter 'hello',
at this thief of treasures of long ago.
It looks up and takes a timeless bow,
when it does so my life ceases to flow.
You greedy alchemist of time and tears!
Your shoulders are trembling at the weight of my years.
The perfume of your sweat, full of yearning, of lack,
it's always been you forcing me forth and back.

There was a ghost that followed my trail,
it's fallen behind with no wind in its sail.
I turn around and wave my hand,
at the glinting grains in the golden sand.

Steffen List

NOT BY CHOICE

Let me be

I am not short nor thin by choice,
But because of the water buckets
I carried day in and day out back in the
Land of the dead,
back home,
Not by choice either, but for survival.

I am not dirty nor black by choice
Nor by the hot sun that burns my body each day.
I was born black, I will die black.
At least this gives me a sense of belonging, not by choice.
My umbilical cord is buried here, in Africa, Africa my roots.
No matter how far I fly, this remains my home and my life.
History is not complete without the land of the Braves.

I am not dull nor ignorant.
My mindset is narrowed and limited,
Not by choice but because of less education
And the little exposure I got.
I was educated under a tree and wrote on the ground.
I crossed valleys with bullets in my face, not by choice,
But in the name of freedom.

My eyes can't altar no word,
My body can't say much either,
But the wounds and scars on my body can tell a story.
The palms of my hands are hardened, my feet have cracked, not by choice
But for survival.

Saara Kalumbu

I am Naked

What did they do to me?
I am stripped of my
Roots
Dignity
Self-respect.
Barbers introduced,
Turned my head into a mirror but,
They grow and sell theirs to me.
My flat stable black foot
Squeezed into an unstable high hill.
My beautiful black shiny face,
Is an ugly transformation of a chemical destruction.
Grandfather's Knobkierie
Turned into AK47.
My *Ombimbi*[1] turned into a salute
In a khaki outfit.
My pride and self-respect turned into inferiority.
I am a victim of circumstances.

Edwin Jackson Tjazerua

---

1   Ovaherero tribal dance performed by warriors before a battle or a celebration of a victory.

Racial Hatred, Breeds Hatred

Wave of nausea strikes

Heavy pain melts into solid injury

Worry till it injures my feelings

Comforting thoughts evaporate quickly from my mind

Racial hatred, it's a growing worry

My head thick with thunderous hatred

Black against the light

Dirty white depiction

Couldn't fake being Mr Nice Guy

Even if I tried to, almost always

It creeps, it drifts back in

Its own shadow beyond my reach

Have chosen to smile in my voice

None drawn on my face

Indication of hatred on a larger scale

Offensively racially flammable

Secretly hidden, in the

Torn cracks beneath my skin

Acceptance of living with hatred

Without hating myself

Dishing out bitter forgiveness.

Ijama Tjivikua

Side by side
(Centre for Cerebral Palsy in Namibia)

I didn't choose
these crooked legs
never in the sun will run

but, side by side my precious friend
we can help each other mend.

I didn't choose
these sightless eyes
never to see my Mother's face

but, side by side we can stand
and we can share a helping hand.

I didn't choose
a world of silence
Father's voice is just a dream

but, side by side my friend so true
we can help each other through.

I didn't choose
to not be able
to tell my Mom I love her so

but, side by side we can be brave
with every bit of love we gave.

I didn't choose
this fractured frame
the prison of my spirit be
but, side by side with you my friend
we can help this whole world mend.

Although my friend I had no choice,
still I live and feel and love
and in the sadness of this world
you can choose to be a friend
and side by side I'll help you mend.

Meraai

Book of Hunger: Chapter One

My friend is the only constant
In the villages and slums of the inner city
Where jail cells are reserved for petty criminals
Driven by empty stomachs.

I have known her all my life
She is a childhood friend
Or a permanent scar
That has shaped my destiny.

She comes in countless forms
And in diverse shapes and sizes
At times resembling marathon athletes
And others who live on a meal per day.

And then there is the starvation of the poor
For whom fasting is not a choice
A hunger so deep and corrosive
That it penetrates the soul and feeds on the spirit.

Here comes the unwanted intruder
Mocking us, even in our sleep
'Food-mares' we call them
The dreams of food that will never materialize.

It is a beautiful monster
That can possess a man
And drive him to a world beyond ethics
Where bread alone is king.

We are products of that eroding hunger
Which feeds on the flesh of man
And produces zombies
Who will slay to make a killing/living?

Hunger speaks
When the stomach growls
I know the lingo,
I can write the book.

Kuhepa Tjondu

The Other Side of Independence Avenue

They tell me that's where my dreams will come true
Not here in Khomasdal
Not in Wanaheda

They say I must go to the small places
With the big houses
Kleine Kuppe. Klein Windhoek.

I must leave these big places
With the small houses.

Wrong side of Independence Avenue
Ergo, wrong side of independence.

The other side

Where the price of one meal,
could feed me for a month

They say that's where independence is
On the other side of Independence Avenue
The right side.

They say my house on Katutura's Luxury Hill
Is on the wrong Luxury Hill
Because it's on the wrong side of Independence Avenue

But these Soweto streets
These streets on the wrong side of Independence Avenue
They raised me
They birthed these dreams I am now told need to be moved
To the right side of Independence Avenue
before they can come true.

Munukayumbwa (Mimi) Mwiya

sentient white bones

their cries can be heard even today
screaming at how their lives were prematurely halted
hanged unjustly from any tree
bayonetted for being Herero or Nama
bang bang bullets into their heads and chest
like shooting birds of game
the flesh died but the bones remain
even today as white as they are
they are sentient white bones
they will rest only when their cries have been heeded
crying for justice to prevail
sentient white bones scattered all over plains
crying for a proper burial
desiring one day all should be well

Coletta Kandimiri

It Never Happened

It's a sad Wednesday afternoon,
the sun's rays are casting their gentle light on your gloomy face because
you can't play with the other children.
Your grandmother was just supposed to sew your broken arm
from when you fell from the Baobab tree in the backyard.
Now she's talking about mending your heart too.
"Your heart is too heavy from the sadness." She says.
"One day it's going to crack your ribs,
it is going to crack your back.
One day it's going to crack your neck."
But the needle keeps breaking.
She sends your brother to the China shop on the corner
but they don't have your colour in stock and school
resumes in three days but the old radio keeps playing the same
old sad tune
So you run half way across the village to your aunt's house
to borrow the magic calabash
to sew your heart back together.
But when you look in your
aunt's eyes you realize there is a residue of the
genocide in all the old people you meet
but they never talk about it
because if the Germans say it never happened
you're still a child, YOU'RE NOT ALLOWED
TO SPEAK OF THE TRAUMA you've never encountered.
Your bones were raised on cow's milk, they are not supposed
to be brittle but nothing is ever that simple.
So you swallow the sadness and you go back to school
and it breaks your heart, cracks it wide open
no sewing machine can mend that type of hurt.
It is generational and it never happened.

Veripuami Nandeekua Kangumine

Pushed

I've been pushed,
Pushed into the unknown
My zone empty
The ruthless golden Kalahari welcomed me,
The meerkat as immediate neighbour
Green pastures degraded into desert
My wooden kraal replaced by iron bars
My bright laughter turned to tears
My happiness into fear
My place filled by a fearless intruder
Turning my kings into slaves.
Pushed, pushed to my limits
With one distinct order
Erase!

Edwin Jackson Tjazerua

LOVE,
IS BUT A HARMONY

Freequential

Detract from me a melody, so that
my soul will whisper and thunder
at the infinite variety of your touch
A myriad play in black and white, be it
naked, unwritten and unmemorised
here under my wing strung in endless rhyme
Eighty-eight steps down a soft-hammered spine
mend your pace and play it your part, listen
the resonance of a free sounding heart –
frequential freedom layered in octaves of truth
to distract and protect from the tragedy
Detract from me all you're about to be, for
Love, is but a harmony

Steffen List

Falling in Love

There is something magical
About meeting a human being
You did not know in the morning
Then feeling like you grew up in the same village.
That is how it felt, for me.

There was no topic that was strange, off-limits or dull
There were no references that needed explanations
Memories of past events intersected
Really, feeling like we knew each other from way back then.
That is how it felt, for me

There was no divide then, I forgot I was far from home
If anything I felt as if I had come back home after a brief visit
The evening was transformed, hours going by
Like meeting kin after an unwelcome separation.
That is how it felt, for me

There is absolutely something surreal
About connecting in a foreign land
That begins to belong to you
When you meet that human being from the same village.
It's how it felt for me

Hannah H. Tarindwa

Love

Love, it is bitter
Makes you carry a burden
But it is beautiful
I hate it
It hurts
But it's handsome
It is careless
Cruel
But very cute
It's painful
But precious,
That's love

Richard Jaar

Together Forever

You are the one
Don't even for one second think
We will never be together
You stole my everything
Tears, pain and frowns
You replaced with
The laughter, smiles and cheers
Lately, many things have been missing
Yet you brought them into my life
I never needed the drama and quarrels
You made sure I did not get any of that
I deserve better and again like always
I received your best
I mean, I don't remember a day
I never did anyway.
You mattered so much to me.
(Now Read From Bottom To The Top)

Wilhelmina Lumbu Kalapungame Iimene

An Ode To Ex's Next Ex

Dear Future Mrs B
Do you think he misses me?
Do you ever feel that sometimes when he looks at you, it's me he hopes to see?

Maybe
Maybe not
Either way, just a thought

Does he look at you the way he looked at me?
With those lovesick eyes
That could make a heart bleed?

Do you think he loves you like he loved me?
And if not, it's not your fault.
Just that mine is a high score to beat

One last thing, Future Mrs B
Do you think he's over me?
If not, then please tell him it's about damn time he is.

Mupalo Mazala

Valour

She wears it on her shoulder
Like a badge of honour
A shiny medal
Of her service and her valour

A pile stacked high
On the shelf of her mind
The taste of her achievements
Linger on her tongue

Ready to be stated
And then celebrated
For only then can her longing be sated

Ready to be sated
But let's hope he never states it
That the honey that drips from her lips has already been tasted

She wears it on her shoulder
That weight of a boulder
That chipped medal
Of all her failed conquests

A mouldy old wooden chest
Of messy old incidents
Tucked away beneath the folds
Of the holes in her heart

The excuse for her melancholy
The tone her sorrow sung
Of a song sealed between her teeth
Where they meet to bite her tongue

Mupalo Mazala

What I Can Do

I can't give you my heart
But it can beat for you.

I can't give you my body
But can give you my touch.

I can't give you my life
But can live for you.

I can't give you my tears
But can cry for you.

Nathaniel Shashi Rufinus

Wish I had known

The good times were really good
In the beginning an all-weather friend, patient and charming
A day would hardly pass without exchanging pleasantries
Used to long for each other like teenagers in love
A lot used to admire what we had as a lot also loathed
Travelled places and drank copious amounts of alcohol
Slept wherever we could put our heads
Endured the sun scorched northern plains
Tolerated the Zambezi valley mosquitoes
Enjoyed the coastal plains and the Namib Desert sand dunes
Weathered the economic cyclones
You were the future in the past
We had big dreams
Of travelling even further than we had traversed
Yet suddenly all failed spectacularly
Arguments became chronic over tiny matters
And suddenly you vanished with no farewells
Was it the unsaid assumptions?
The underlying apprehensions?
The not knowing that became a slow motion to catastrophe?
What grave psychological disturbances warranted such?
Was it the fear of hardship, hunger or loneliness?
Wish I had listened to those signs and cries
Thought you would be fine as in those smiling social media photos
Never anticipated you could just leave me a bag of confusion
A mess of a soul guilty of being the cause
Of your flight from this existence
Everything coming down like the Twin towers
Multitudes of questions only you could have answered
Wish I had known.

Charles Mlambo

Where the ocean meets the desert

The desert loved the ocean with a passion
Fell in love with the sensuality of her waves
Allowed her volatility to try to quench his fiery desire
Every day she would reach out to him
Allowed her water to graciously linger long enough to show him her love
But the moon wouldn't permit her
He controlled her every move
Too jealous to allow her, he dragged her back
Vindictively the moon enlisted the help of man
Manipulated them into building a road to separate the two loves
The ocean reaches herself out everyday
Too heartbroken to welcome the embrace of insanity

Jacobina Kalunduka

These vessels

For years it has been brewing.
Behold, an overflow!
Rivers and oceans now burst forth;
Living waters.
We are vessels,
Never broken in vain.
Unlike damaged goods,
We are not beyond repair.
We are pressed to release a light for ages hidden,
To show others that we are not hopeless.
Where the echo of agony reverberates,
We are microphones of His comfort,
Amplifiers of His love.
We are vessels,
Never broken in vain.
Unlike damaged goods,
We are not beyond repair.
We are broken to show that if we too can be stitched,
Then we all can be mended;
By love true and love pure.
We are not abandoned.
We know mercy,
We know grace.
Redemption?
Story of our lives.

Julia N. T. Nekomba

DUST OF GLORY

Forgotten Royalty

My bloodline is forgotten royalty
Seers
Warriors
Kings
And Queens.
We reigned on the banks of rivers.
Remnant memories
Flood my dreams
I remember on your behalf
Golden sceptres and mango trees
Mountain song in ancient tongue
Opening gateways to prophesy.
Many have fallen asleep
But I oh I was born free
I bring with me gold, myrrh and chamomile tea
Worship
And the dust of glory.

Zemha Gawachas

Birth right

I was born
with a spoon of sand
in my mouth.

So I swallowed
and tasted the blood
bubbling and boiling
thicker than water
but thinner than the love
trickling to the cracked skin of my soul
where fallen seeds of the sun
sprouted thorny wire wings

not pretty, but durable enough
to carry me away and back
to my roots in the sand.

Sylvia Schlettwein

My heritage

I'm not called by anything which identifies me,
but if I were,
If I had an African name
It would be long.
It would signal the longevity of my heritage,
The everlasting and undeniable royalty of my roots.
My African name would signal strength –
Bedazzled with the boldest vowels and consonants,
It would be the tongue twister others would feign to despise,
and yet practise because of its importance.
It would be like a melody of the richest nature – sounding as
Graceful as the steps of young girls dancing round the fire.
My African name would inspire love – *ohole, uthando, zuvero…*
Just like home.
I'm not called by anything which identifies me,
but my identity is engraved in the uniqueness of my skills, my boldness, in my warmth.
They all scream out 'African Child'
and that is my heritage.

Remaliah Margarida Chingufo

Ode to Negritude

Two eyes
One mouth, sensuous
Succulent to behold
one flat nose
Kinky hair, brown eyes
Dark chocolate they come
So lovely
Titillating to behold
Dark brown to mulatto
Zebra clan, monkey clan
Rhino clan, fish clan
Travelled the same road
The colonial route
Same tongue
Bantu tongue
The African flavour
One we are, together as one
Tolerance brings unity
Africa for Africans
Africans for Africa

Nelson Mlambo

Perm Blues

These strings are strong and healthy,
their roots so deep
You can tell I take care of mine.
I am black,
woman if that wasn't enough to alert you
I am proud.
Meme worked on my crown
till I was old enough to pay attention
to how I wanted it worn
She taught me how to nurture it,
to let no one disrespect it.
How dare you come and try strip that away from me.
I perm my hair because I can
I am not washing away my tribal strains or
Straitening my heritage out
This is not what history meant when it said we were suppressed.
I perm my hair because I want and it shouldn't make me less than
Natural.
Nor does it conceal my identity.

Maria-Oo Haihambo

We Africans

What are we?
We Africans
Who wear our 'African dress'
Like costumes on special occasion.

Who are we?
We Africans
Who only eat African food at cultural festivals?
'You are what you eat'.

Are you Aware?
You Africans
Who have mastered English, French and Portuguese,
That there is power in the mother tongue?

And to you Africans
I pray, I say and I ask
Whose Gods do you worship?
And where are the black Gods?

What shall it profit an African,
If he should travel the world
and cross the seven seas
Without seeing the Nile valley?

(Inspired by Aime Cesaire and Thomas Sankara)

Kuhepa Tjondu

Wild Africa

The fading sunset is calling
The violet dawn is falling
Bushveld creatures disappear
A chorus of singing crickets is all I can hear
The jackal calls to his friends
The leaves dance with the wind, as the tree bends
Bright light spills over the savannah as the sun breaks through
Grass coated with silver from the morning dew
Rainbow birds fly over a buffalo herd
The tears in my eyes make this scene blurred
Tribal drums your beating heart
From this continent I would never part
Wild Africa pure and true,
My heart is one with you

Lize-Mari de Bod

I am Africa

I am more than the colour of my people.

I am every shade, from the purest of white to the darkest of black.

I am the warm glow of the sunsets on the horizon.

I am the blues and greens of the shore as they kiss the desert.

I am the roar of a male lion as he calls out his claim.

I am the melody of the birds in the early mornings.

I am Africa

I am more than the colour of my people.

I am the laughter of little white kneed children as they run in the dusty streets.

I am the laughter of families seated around the fire sharing ancient stories.

I am the scared looks on little faces as they are told horror tales by their grandfathers.

I am the sound of running feet as they chase animals across the fields.

I am the smile on a grey haired woman as she looks down on her children.

I am the delicious smells of traditional foods at a family gathering.

I am Africa

I am more than the colour of my people.

I am the heart of my people.

I am the kindness of my mothers.

I am the pride and strength of my fathers.

I am the innocence of my children.

I am the wisdom of my elders.

I am Africa.

Davency Mbaha

ABOUT THE POETS

Martha Sibila ǀKhoëses is a Namibian storyteller. Poetry is her passion as she sees it as a language in its own right. In pursuit of her writing career, Martha obtained a Bachelor's degree in English from the Namibia University of Science and Technology and is currently studying towards a postgraduate qualification at the same institution. She has self-published four books and works as a teacher in Language and Information and Communications Technology (ICT). Her passion for creative writing has seen her writing diverse content including poetry chapbooks, an inspirational memoir, an Afrikaans romantic novel and a traditional ǂNu-khoen novel. Martha is a mother of two and grandmother residing in Okahandja.

Aquila Bartholomeus (AKA Priscilla Akukothela) was born and raised in Windhoek, where she started writing at an early age. It wasn't until 2016, however, that she took writing more seriously, albeit as a hobby. Writing mostly short stories and poetry, she is inspired by everyday life experiences of both herself and her loved ones. An avid runner and fitness enthusiast, her style of writing follows that of free style and prose and she writes mostly on the topics of love, self-acceptance, positive body image and mental health.

Batchotep (AKA Batcho Katumbo) see Batcho Katumbo.

Bronwen A. Beukes (Bock) graduated from Dr Lemmer High School in 1989, and obtained a BA and education degree at the Academy in Windhoek before returning to her old school to teach English. Her passion for the magic of language inspires her writing about the meaning and value of life, human fears and triumphs, and the challenges and pleasures of love. She became an Education Officer at the National Institute for Educational Development (NIED) in 2002, joined Namibia University of Science and Technology (NUST) in 2005, obtained a Master's degree in Linguistics in 2010 and has lectured in the English Section at the University of Namibia (UNAM) since 2012.

Remaliah Margarida Chingufo, a medical student at the University of Namibia, was raised in Mozambique, and has a great passion for art. Remaliah (Hebrew for 'The exaltation of God') writes poems about her beliefs, passions and doubts for two reasons: the first and least important being that she did not succeed in composing daily diary entries. The second and most significant reason was that writing poems helped Remaliah notice changes in her thought patterns, helping the "born-free" track her mental growth. As time went by, poetry became a lifestyle. She believes poetry is found in various, even unknown forms such as dance.

Crispin D. P. Clay was born and raised in Zambia, went to school in South Africa and Zimbabwe, graduated in Wales in 1967, taught English at Centaurus High School in Windhoek from 1970 to 1973, married a Namibian teacher and moved to Lüderitz to write. He ran a retail business for 39 years, during which time he was deeply involved in the Lüderitzbucht Foundation's efforts to promote the town, helping to arrange the Centenary Festival in 1983 and the Dias Festival in 1988. He retired in 2012 and stays busy with Lüderitz projects. He is currently working on a book of stories, photos and poems connected to Dias. It keeps expanding.

Lize-Mari de Bod is 18 years old and has been writing poetry since the age of 14, drawn to African nature and society as themes. People's behaviour and the depth of their purpose is what interests Lize-Mari to unravel the secrets of society that are out in the open but require a unique perspective. 'Wild Africa' expresses the passion that the poet has for her land, and her appreciation of living in paradise. Lize-Mari believes that through poetry we can learn deeper emotions and explore other realms in the poetry itself, from reality to a dream world.

André du Pisani, who holds a PhD in Philosophy from the University of Cape Town, retired at the end of 2013 as Professor of Politics at the University of Namibia. In 2006 the French Government awarded him a Palme Academique for his contribution to public conversation. From 2013-2017, André was a member of a Global Reflection Group that explored 'The Monopoly on the Use of Force'. He is also a photographic artist, collector of visual art, a published poet and a rock art enthusiast.

Hugh Ellis was born in Windhoek and grew up in London, where his parents were in exile from Namibia, returning to the country after independence in 1990. As a reporter for *The Namibian* newspaper from 2000 to 2003, and later as a freelance journalist and UN communication officer, he saw both positive and negative sides of Namibian society. Hugh obtained an MA in journalism and media studies from Rhodes University and a PhD in media studies from Wits University. He currently lectures at the Namibia University of Science and Technology. Hugh started writing poetry in 1998, and has been a regular performer at Spoken Word performance poetry events in Windhoek.

Anne-Marie Issa Brown Garises strives to achieve greatness both academically and artistically. She is currently learning Mandarin Chinese at the University of Namibia and is the curator of the municipal museum of Keetmanshoop. Apart from poetry, Issa also writes prose, inspired by the book titled *If You Want to Write* (2011/1938) by Brenda

Ueland. Ms Ueland had this to say, "...if you really want to write poems; you should write from your heart. Readers should be emotional after reading your poems. And if you are lucky you will have readers ... that listen to what you have to say and believe in what you just said". Issa wants that.

Zemha Gawachas hails from Mariental and holds a Bachelor of Jurisprudence and an Honours degree in law. She is an aspiring diplomat, motivational speaker, poet and an ardent lover of literature. She is also the founder of Tare-khoe Elevation which literally translates to "women elevation". Tare-khoe Elevation is a project based organisation which seeks to create synergies, connecting women from different walks of life to each other across demographics, in the hope of forming a sisterhood and support system, fostering resilience and providing learning experiences through story telling.

Mercy George is studying for a Bachelor of Arts degree in English at the University of Namibia. Mercy's love for literature began in her early years when her mother, who was an English teacher, would read to her and encouraged her to expand her reading interests. Upon completion of her studies, she aspires to be a lecturer in literature. Her hobbies include learning about other cultures, watching films, hiking and writing. Though Mercy has been writing since she was younger, this is her first published work.

Dalene Gous is an amateur poet who writes her best work from a place of emotional turmoil. The original English poem 'It's Raining without Water' was written in 1997, after the sudden death of her younger brother in an accident. After her marriage in 2002, her father-in-law, S. F. Gous, translated the poem into Afrikaans.

Maria-Oo Haihambo is currently studying at the University of Namibia. She has a curious mind and a dry sense of humour that often lands her in unwanted predicaments. She struggles with insecurities about writing which she is currently trying to conquer by performing to audiences in settings like Spoken Word Namibia and Open Mic. Some of her writing embodies pain and trauma while projecting self-love internally. In a society where violation of women and children is increasing, she believes it is important to educate the boy child and the adult male in the valuing and treatment of women, and to reject the standards of beauty society places upon women.

Tessa Harris was born and raised in Windhoek. She is a writer and poet currently at the Centre for New Writing, University of Manchester as a Commonwealth PhD candidate, researching the formal techniques used in the combinations of text and image in narrative work. Tessa has had short stories and poetry published in Namibia, South Africa and the UK.

Dianne Hubbard was born in the United States, gaining a degree in English from the University of North Carolina and a law degree from Harvard Law School. She then acquired a degree in English (Hons) from Stellenbosch University in South Africa. Dianne first came to Namibia to gather information for Lawyers' Committee on Human Rights (now Human Rights First) and has lived in Windhoek since 1989. She has served as Coordinator of the Gender Research & Advocacy Project of the Legal Assistance Centre since February 1993, where her work focuses on gender-based violence, family law and children's rights. Married to Adv. Andrew Corbett, she has two children, Kelsey and Jason.

Wilhelmina Lumbu Kalapungame Iimene is a 20 year old Namibian girl. She was raised in Iikokola-Elombe village, attended primary school at Lano Private School and matriculated from Oshigambo High School. The current NUST student loves and is passionate about writing poetry and novels. In 2017, she published her first novel titled *Not All Secrets Keep People Together* and her second book *Poetry From Within* in 2018. Besides writing, she enjoys playing netball, keeping fit and watching series. She is an intelligent young girl who sees everything from a positive perspective and is always eager to break new ground because she believes that it is possible if she puts her heart to it.

Kina Indongo is a Namibian media student, artist, poet and blogger, born to elderly parents who spent their youth fighting for Namibia's liberation, the circumstances of which are reflected in the thoughtful, personal and pan-Africanist sentiments of her poetry. Kina's poetry has been influenced by the exhilarating honesty in the works of female African poets such as Warsan Shire, Ijeoma Umebinyuo, Nayirah Waheed and Yrsa Daley Ward who inspired her to express the mundane, private and tragic parts of African life, particularly the realities of those in Namibia. Her work employs short descriptions of familiar scenarios and circumstances in a manner that provokes a pause to reconsider the state of affairs.

Omaano Itana is a Namibian based writer and Spoken Word poet who began her creative work from the age of 12. She explores the human condition and her writing is an intimate look at the personal relationships one has with the world, examining life, love, loss and longing in a way that is both melancholic and hopeful. She was afforded the opportunity to perform one of her poems 'Caged at a prison' in Windhoek. The way the inmates allowed their tears to flow was an experience she'll never forget. Omaano believes that by sharing her own fears, doubts and struggles she can help others grow out of their cocoons.

Richard Jaar, born in Mariental in 1989, spent his childhood in Gibeon where he completed primary and high school. Like many youths, Richard did not score grades good enough to continue tertiary education so he enrolled with the Namibian College of Open Learning (NAMCOL) to upgrade his grade 12 symbols. Richard holds a certificate in Accounting and Finance (Level 4). He has worked as a General Worker (labourer), peer educator, literacy promotor, driver and polling officer. Currently, Richard is serving a 15 year sentence for murder at Hardap Correctional Facility, already having served four years. Richard loves reading poems and that encourages him to write his own.

Kerry Jones is a linguist and activist for mother tongue education in Khoesan languages in southern Africa. The poem featured in this anthology, 'Shshsh listen...' reflects her observations made in the winter of 2018 in Nyae Nyae and surrounds. Chief Tsamkxao ≠Oma, the traditional leader of the Juǀ'hoansi in the Nyae Nyae conservancy, asked that Tsoan (Dr Jones' Juǀ'hoan name) carry this message to Windhoek and the outside world. "Namibians need to know what is happening in Tsumkwe and in Nyae Nyae. There is enough land for all. We have fought hard for our land and our people. Our rights must be protected, and the time is now."

Saara Kadhikwa is a creative who finds poetry therapeutic. She read Environmental Biology at the University of Namibia. She is looking forward to delving into Linguistics and Literature in the near future.

Kavevangua Kahengua was born in central Botswana at a village called Mosu. He is a descendant of the Ovaherero who sought refuge in Botswana during the German wars of 1904–7. He grew up listening to his grandmother's stories. Upon returning to Namibia, he attended creative writing workshops at the University of Namibia. He contributed poems to *The Inner Eye: Namibian Poetry in Process* (1997) and *In search of questions: A Collection of New Namibian Poems* (2005), both published by Basler Afrika Bibliographien, Basel. As sole writer, Kahengua has published *Dreams* (2002) and *Invoking voices: An Anthology of Poems* (2012), both published by Namibia Publishing House, Windhoek.

Saara Kalumbu was born on the 23rd of October 1997. She was nursed on artificial milk and raised under harsh conditions, being disciplined with a belt. She ate with her hands, often getting only a single meal a day. Determined to go to school, she walked long distances and studied on the ground by candlelight. In 2016 she moved to the city, to go to school in a cab and type on a computer under city lights. With a face shiny with Vaseline and poverty in her veins, she is determined to fight for her unknown future.

157

Jacobina Kalunduka is a 19-year-old student who aspires to be an author one day. The phrase "Dynamite comes in small packages" best describes her. Her height should never fool you. She spends the majority of her time reading and writing. Her family and friends are the most important people to her.

Marco Kalunduka is an amateur poet. His alter ego is Taliban as it represents what the Taliban stood for in the 1990s, a struggle of the common folk against imperialism. Marco had a happy childhood but grew to be a pessimist, a hollow shelled young man. Now his focus is on dark (usually) and profoundly morbid poetry. His favourite rock band is Breakin Benjamin; he finds their rich, pain-riddled lyrics inspire some of his best work.

Tulipomwene Kalunduka is a passionate, ambitious 18 year old who craves to rattle and shake up this world through her loving spirit. She is an extroverted enthusiast who works to inspire all those around her through her speech and writing. She loves anything creative, as it challenges her artsy self. She is God-fearing and not afraid to stand up for her beliefs. Her writing first started in her early years at Windhoek High School, which has been reflected in her articles for the *Namibian Sun* newspaper, her poetry recitals and talent show performances. She hopes that her compassionate love and her leadership style leave footprints behind her. She loves life.

Coletta Kandimiri is a PhD candidate from the University of Namibia and a member of the Windhoek Writer's Club. Her writing of poetry and prose is shaped by her contact with other people as well as her personal experiences and exposure to a variety of writings. The idea of storytelling motivates her, for story telling encompasses teaching and entertaining which are indeed part of human socialisation. Coletta believes that writing down one's thoughts actually immortalises them; they will live even after the writer is long gone.

Veripuami Nandeekua Kangumine is a 22 year old woman who was born in Ovitoto but grew up in Windhoek. Veripuami was raised by her grandmother who inspires most of her poetry. As a young girl, she would watch her grandmother with intense admiration as she did her cooking or pulled weeds from her garden. In attempting to describe the emotions her grandmother evoked in her, she grew to love words. She regards poetry to be the language of the soul and loves performing her poems and writing. Veripuami wants to help others by telling her story through poetry so that others can heal from issues of abandonment and lack of self-love.

Batcho Katumbo (AKA Batchotep) is a 28 year old man born and bred in Mondesa, Swakopmund. He is currently pursuing a medical degree in Cuba. He holds a BSc in

Animal Sciences from the University of Namibia. The highlights of his poetry career are unquestionably reciting the poem 'I am Sam Nujoma' for the founding President Dr Sam Nujoma during his visit to Cuba in September 2016, and 'Dream of Dawn' at the 40th Cassinga commemoration in Havana, Cuba, in the presence of the Vice President, Dr Nangolo Mbumba. The purpose of his poetry is to educate, motivate and to help preserve Namibian history deemed inconsequential by mainstream reporters and historians.

Martha Sibila |Khoëses see first entry p. 153.

Steffen List is a Namibian artist specialising in the visual arts with a primary interest in illustration and the multi-faceted world of graphic design. He has spent the last 15 years working for the creative sector in Namibia, South Africa, France, Germany, the UK, Switzerland and the USA. A constant thirst for fulfilment and purpose in and through his work as well as for growth as an artist, has made his focus inclusive of the writing and performing of music, seeing the release of his first 'EP' in 2013. He is also working towards his first solo exhibition.

Prince Kamaazengi Marenga is a fierce Pan-Afrikan Poet. Ngũgĩ Wa Thiong'o's words regarding a person without consciousness being lost and "easily guided by another to wherever the guide wants to take him..." have strengthened his ache for self-graduation in his quest for knowledge. He is co-author of the collection of poems *Peri Nawa Uriri* (Chief Keharanjo II's Poetry Factory) in loving memory of Chief Keharanjo Nguvauva II. Prince worked as a researcher and translator on the documentary film 'Waterberg to Waterberg' (MaMoKoBo Video & Research 2014); at the Pan Afrikan Centre of Namibia as a media consultant, and for *The Southern Times* as a freelance journalist. He performs regularly at the Goethe Institute under Township Production.

Mupalo Mazala is a Zambian born aspiring writer who holds a Bachelor's degree in English from the Namibia University of Science and Technology. She has lived in Windhoek for the past seven years where she plans to further her studies in the field of literature.

Davency Mbaha is a 23 year old young lady with a wild imagination and a brain that never stops thinking. She grew up in a small village in Okakarara surrounded by the love of a widowed mother and five siblings. Davency moved to Otjiwarongo to complete high school at Paresis Secondary School in 2011, after which she spent four years in Malaysia studying Advertising and Design at Multimedia University. During that time she gave in to her passion for writing which is not limited to poems. When she is not reading or writing, she indulges in her love for food or listening to music.

Christelize Elleen Meintjies is a 14 year old ninth grade student. She was born in Keetmanshoop and currently lives in Aranos. She has shown interest in literature from a young age and represents her unique perspective on life in her poetry, always striving to convey a positive message in everything she writes. Christelize chooses to see beauty in everything and believes that perseverance, courage and kindness conquers all. Her work deals with her real life experiences and emotions. Her broad horizons and imagination are visible in every word. Christelize aspires to become a published poet and author.

Meraai (AKA Ria Kotze) is a barefoot child of the Namib with too many words in her head. *Vlinderkind,* her first attempt at publishing, received an award from the Afrikaans Language and Culture Association (ATKV) in 2017. A selection from this work was published in *Stemme uit Namibië 1* and a further eight in *Stemme uit Namibië 2,* with over 90% of the total coming from her writer's blog, *Die Namib Skryf.* Ria received another two ATKV recommendations for poetry and a short story in 2019. With no formal literary education, she writes out of love for her language and to purify her heart. She enjoys pokerwork, burning poetry, psalms, portraits or motorcycles into leather.

Valery Mkabeta is a wife, a daughter, a mother, a sister and a friend. She works as an administrative assistant and writing is her hobby. She loves the power of words, teaching and conversations. She does her best writing on mountain tops, in the bathroom and backyard gardens. Valery loves to play medieval matchmaker of soul and words on the journey of self-discovery, transporting readers to a place where the bold heroes have endearing flaws, the women are stronger than they look, the land is lush and untamed, and chivalry is alive and well!

Charles Mlambo was born in Zimbabwe and came to Namibia in 2000 as a young professional librarian, working at Ongwediva Teachers' Resource Centre in the north of Namibia. He was instrumental in the establishment of public libraries in Okahao and Outapi. From 2004, he was Senior Librarian for the National Library of Namibia. Now a permanent resident of Namibia, Charles is currently the Chief Librarian at the National Library of Namibia. Educated at Harare Polytechnic, Zimbabwe and the University of South Africa (UNISA), he is currently pursuing post graduate studies with Stellenbosch University in the field of Knowledge Management. He is a keen reader who writes in his spare time.

Nelson Mlambo has degrees from the University of Namibia, the University of Zimbabwe and Stellenbosch University. He is a Senior Lecturer at the University of Namibia and loves teaching poetry. He is also the Chairman of the UNAM Press Editorial Board.

160

Jane Mungabwa is a Namibian poet and scriptwriter. She has graced local Spoken Word poetry stages and wrote a script for an educational Namibian comic book titled, *Kasi-wise: info beats the hustle.* Jane is passionate about English language learning and teaching, and she aspires to publish a variety of books that can used for local English language teaching. Jane is also a human rights activist who is part of the ACTION Namibia Coalition, an organisation that is actively lobbying government for the promulgation and implementation of an access to information law in Namibia.

Munukayumbwa (Mimi) Mwiya is a floater who sometimes sits still enough to write. She is Namibian.

Esther Nantana is a 22 year old from Ongwediva who writes for the purpose of coping and dealing with emotions. She never uses the terms 'poet' or 'writer' to describe herself. She instead describes herself as someone who has so much to say that she found an additional outlet through writing.

Nandu Ndabeni, known simply as Ricky by peers and acquaintances, has been a poet since the age of twelve. He is an outspoken individual, and poetry provides him with a platform to express himself in words. Through reading novels and short stories, he developed a love for literature and throughout the years he has challenged himself to grow and develop different styles to his poetic work. He is at peace with pen and paper. He writes in the moment. To him, poetry should be used as a tool to narrate life's experiences and preserve memories. Poetry has and will continue to be an integral part of Ricky's day to day life.

Beauty Ndapanda is a Namibian poet. Her poetic style is lyrical and contemporary. She writes poems focusing on introspective topics, subconscious emotions, relationships and philosophies of life. Poetry is her talent and passion.

Gloria Ndilula is a freelance writer and has been writing since the age of nine: short comic strips for friends, short stories or novellas. At 14, she entered poems in the 'Be A Star Performer' competition, not only winning a Gold for her work, but the Best Overall in the Creative Writing category. Creativity comes naturally to Gloria as she is also a photographer (Namibian Nomad Photography).

Julia Nekomba is an aspiring Chartered Accountant, currently busy with her training program at Price Waterhouse Cooper. She has a fierce passion for the arts, especially poetry and music. Her writing covers diverse aspects of life, intending to reach out and transform lives in a way that is fascinating and entertaining.

Rémy Ngamije is a Rwandan-born Namibian short story writer, essayist, columnist, poet, and the author of *The Eternal Audience of One*, his debut novel published by Blackbird Books (2019). He also writes for brainwavez.org, a writing collective based in South Africa. He is the editor-in-chief of Namibia's first literary magazine: *Doek!* His short stories have appeared in *Litro Magazine*, *AFREADA*, *The Johannesburg Review of Books*, *The Amistad*, *The Kalahari Review*, *American Chordata*, *Doek!*, and *Azure*. More of his writing can be read on his website: remythequill.com

Anneli Nghikembua lectures in the Department of Communication at Namibia University of Science and Technology (NUST). In 2013 she published an anthology of poems titled *A True me In Words* (MacMillan Education Namibia), drawing inspiration from everyday life and stories that relate to her upbringing. Among the top ten best KTV South Africa short story writers, she also won the best Speak Africa short story competition in the Southern African Development Community (SADC), and attended a Speak Africa Conference in Addis Ababa, Ethiopia, where she obtained a certificate in film and digital narratives. She is working on a novel, second poetry anthology, and an English second language handbook, as well as a PhD through Rhodes University.

Job Ndeutapo Nghipandulwa was born in 1996, raised in a single-mother headed family in Oupili village, matriculated from Haimbili Haufiku Secondary school in 2014, and enrolled for an Honours degree in Geology at UNAM. As a child, Job loved to read and he recalls begging librarians to give him more than one book at a time. Introduced to English literature in his grade 11 higher level English class, he was inspired by William Shakespeare and Chinua Achebe. A year later, he wrote his first poem 'Alcohol: A snake in the grass', and a novel 'A friend in need is a friend indeed', which was unfortunately lost with only a chapter to complete.

Freeman Ngulu is a graduate in Media Studies and Political Studies from the University of Namibia. He served on the Campus News as a reporter and has since become a mid-career journalist. His poetry questions his understanding of metaphysics and natural law. Being a media student, he also incorporates cinematic imagery in his work.

Sifiso Nyati is a Namibian novelist, poet and dramatist with long experience in teaching English and didactics of English at the University of Namibia. Nyathi has written many plays including *God of Women* and *Oracle of Cidino* which are taught as part of Namibian literature at UNAM. In addition, Nyathi is the author of a novella, *The Other Presence* and an anthology *Ballads of Insomnia*. He holds a number of graduate and under graduate qualifications from the University of Namibia as well as a Doctoral Degree in applied linguistics and curriculum studies from the University of

Southern Illinois at Carbondale, Illinois, USA. He is an admitted attorney by Namibia's High Court.

Simson Mario Ochurub is a 28 year old Namibian from the Kunene Region. He works as an administrative officer for the Kunene Regional Council, Directorate of Education, Arts and Culture, in Khorixas. Simson is also a motivational speaker, aspiring entrepreneur and author. His first book *Your Plan vs Your Life* (2018; distributed freely in PDF) reflects on how we deviate from our initial plans due to life's challenges. He is currently writing his second book *The Village Girl* to be launched in 2020. Simson believes that through motivational writing projects, he can promote a Namibian culture of reading, not only by reaching out to his local community but to Namibians and readers across the globe.

Tuli Phoenix is a visual artist, as experimental in her work as she is in her crusade to find memorabilia in the scattered vintage stores of Windhoek's secretive corners. Enormously enthusiastic about quirky designs, fine art, so-called awkward personalities and felines, she enriches her life with what she considers knowledge inaccessible to the norm and long lost to the masses. In her work Tuli specialises in creating mixed-media artwork, dressing up in meticulously crafted costumes for her culturally inspired public performances, and creating satirical illustrations. She has exhibited locally, at Art Fairs in both Cape Town and Johannesburg, and at Art Market Budapest.

Klaus Rennack was born in 1946 in northern Germany where he studied English and Geography as subjects for teaching. He became a middle school coordinator and then vice principal at the international German school (iDSB) in Brussels. In 2008 he and his wife Helga Falk moved to Windhoek where he taught and was vice principal for the German school (DHPS). He has always written poetry for private pleasure and played in rock bands from the sixties, being the lead singer in the Namibian rock group Rushour. He created the group Trypoetry (see the website www.trypoetrylove.com) and is currently part of the radio team in the NBC German programme Rockwärtz.

Nathaniel Shashi Rufinus is a grade 9 learner at St Mary's Odibo High School in the north of Namibia. He was born in Tsumeb. His father Gabriel is a big inspiration and role model. He has five siblings, all of whom either dance or are competent athletes. Shashi loves playing soccer and is part of the Ohangwena second division team. He uses his writing to communicate, his number one inspiration being himself. He usually writes what comes from deep within and has many poems yet to be published. Shashi aspires to entertain his audience with poetry to heal the soul and bring happiness to the world, one poem at a time.

Aristides 'Are' Sambiliye is a resident of Walvis Bay. A teacher by profession, he is an avid reader. His love for poetry evolved from his love for Hip Hop music. He writes poems in his spare time whenever the inspiration comes to him. He considers himself an extroverted introvert and writing serves as a catharsis. He hopes one day to have an anthology published.

Sylvia Schlettwein was born in 1975 in Omaruru, central Namibia. She graduated with a BA degree in German and French from the University of Cape Town, and continued to study German and French Language and Literature at the University of Stuttgart and the Ecole Normale Supérieure de Lettres et Sciences Humaines in Lyon, France. After completing her Master's degree, she returned to Windhoek in 2003. Sylvia writes, translates and edits literature in English, German and Afrikaans. She has won several awards for her short stories and poetry and has published two collections of short stories, one in English and one in German. Sylvia lives, loves, works and writes in Windhoek.

Lazarus Shatipamba is a 21 year old Namibian poet born in the north of the country, but bred in the City of Windhoek, cared for by his aunties and grandparents. He graduated in 2016 as President of the Chess Club at Jan Möhr Secondary School. He learnt to read at an early age and has since had a passion for reading and writing. When his nose is not buried in a book, he is most likely learning French, meditating, writing poetry or making sure he is not the worst chess player around. He is grateful for the peace in our beloved country and looks towards the future with hopeful optimism.

Ina-Maria Shikongo was born in Kalulu, Angola and grew up in the former GDR (German Democratic Republic) until 1990. She attended primary and high school in Windhoek. After completing grade 12, she attended the University of Namibia to do a Bachelor of Arts, majoring in Fashion Design and Advertising. In 2001, Ina-Maria obtained a degree in fashion at Lycée Sévigné de Tourcoing in France. On her return, she developed a project called Fusion, teaching a basic introduction to fashion. In 2017, Ina-Maria created an NGO, Eloolo Permaculture Initiative, with two of her colleagues, and now teaches Permaculture at Farm Okukuna in Goreangab. Ina-Maria believes in a fair world for all beings.

Onesmus Shimwafeni is a writer who dares to think out of the box. He is innovative and constantly writes new poems that challenge both the way we think as individuals and as a society. He grew up in Germany, lived in East Africa, South Africa and worked in Shanghai, China. Onesmus quickly realized that writing poems is a God given talent that flows through his blood and started putting it to good use. His poetry is influenced by the world around him.

Sanmari Steenkamp, born in 1974, holds a Master's degree in Clinical Psychology as well as a Professional Diploma in Education from the University of Namibia. She works as a psychologist in Windhoek and her passion for the arts and all forms of creative expression has led to her participation in two Tulipamwe International Artists' Workshops (Namibia). She was chosen as the Country Director for Arts in Medicine Project (2018), a global volunteer project to facilitate creative engagements in medical and human rights spaces, promoting wellbeing and lifting up spirits. Running the AIM Project has led her to a deeper appreciation of creative writing, especially poetry.

Alex Swartbooi was born in Keetmanshoop on the 2nd of May 1994, and raised in Snyfontein where he started primary school. Alex grew up in a religious home, took part in school activities and was head boy at primary school. He attended high school at J. A. Nel Senior Secondary School in Keetmanshoop, where he developed a passion for poetry. He writes poems that inspire his life and is working on a poetry book and a biography. He is currently serving an 8 year sentence for culpable homicide at Hardap Correctional Facility. His dream is to become a sought-after poet.

Hannah H. Tarindwa is a Lecturer in Journalism and Media. She is a Master's student in Monitoring and Evaluation and identifies as a social scientist. She enjoys reading, writing and travelling within Africa. She is the founder of Writers' Academy Namibia and a published poet, including *This Woman Revealed* (2015) available on Amazon. She won her first poetry competition at the age of 14. She is also an academic writer and is working on her first novel. She believes that now is the time for Africans to champion Indigenous Knowledge and to embrace cultural expression. She believes Chinua Achebe's works should be taught in every African high school literature class.

Jacquie Tarr is a Namibian environmental scientist, writer and artist. She was educated in the fields of natural science and education at the Universities of the Witwatersrand and Pietermaritzburg in South Africa. Her creative work is strongly influenced by her love and respect for the natural world. She finds writing poetry challenging and cathartic and uses it to express her awe of nature, the horrors of the environmental crisis and her deep interest in (and confusion regarding) the human condition.

Clementine Tjameya is an English major at the Namibia University of Science and Technology. She comes from Rundu, a small town situated in the north-eastern part of Namibia. She completed her primary education at Sarusungu Combined School, and her secondary education at Rundu Secondary School. She started writing when she was in eighth grade, and her passion for writing has increased. She currently has two books for publication, a children's story and a play. In December 2016 she established a programme called Namibia Writers' Empowerment Programme which aims to encourage aspiring writers. For more information on the programme see https://clementine40.wordpress.com/author/clementinetjameya/

Edwin Jackson Tjivingurura Tjazerua was born in Tses, a small village in southern Namibia. His family was displaced during the Ovaherero/Nama genocide and so he grew up in an Otjiherero-speaking family living in southern Namibia, learning to speak Khoekhoegowab fluently. Edwin taught for several years in southern Namibia and developed a keen interest in the legacy of Ovaherero living in this part of the country, writing poems that narrate his life story and the effects of the 1904–1907 Namibian Genocide. He draws inspiration from Kavevangua Kahengua's *Dreams* and life as an Omuherero born in Botswana. Edwin currently works as a librarian in the Systems Department of the University of Namibia Library.

Magnus Elius Tjiueza, born in the dusty small town of Usakos in the early 1980s currently resides in Walvis Bay (occasionally in Swakopmund). His love for writing was activated in grade 10 when writing poetry and essays took centre stage in his life. He wrote love poems for his classmates and was paid apples and chips during break times in between writing speeches for those who aspired to be LRCs (members of the Learner Representative Council). As is the norm in the universe, work, relocations, children and migrations took effect and his love for writing poetry dwindled. He believes he still has a passion for poetry, however, and has something to offer.

Ijama Tjivikua was born on 2nd July 1998 in Windhoek. He went to school in Gobabis where he gained in knowledge and experience to be more creative in writing poetry. He is committed to expressing his doctrine of psychological reasoning to defend and oppose topics in debate.

Kuhepa Tjondu, the third of seven children, was born and raised in the north-western part of Namibia in Opuwo, Kunene region. Both his parents were Otjiherero language teachers. His maternal grandmother, Uakotoka Tjikotoke, introduced him to stories, songs and poetry. He told his first story at night while seated around the fire in the village of Oukongo. His poetry is influenced by the language and culture of the people of Kaokoland and the Ugandan/South Sudanese poet Taban Lo Liyong, also known as the black sheep of East African literature. Kuhepa's poem 'Truth' was published in England in an anthology titled *Whispers on the breeze* (United Press, 2009). He performs regularly at the Goethe Institute poetry sessions.

Hijenduanao Uanivi is a 21 year-old Ovaherero Namibian male. He began his education in Ongwediva and completed it in Windhoek. Currently, he is a fourth year student at the Namibia University of Science and Technology (NUST), pursuing an engineering degree. He resides with his mother, Glory Nguvauva, stepfather, Justus Nekongo and four of his 13 siblings in Otjomuise's 8de Laan. Exposed to the hardships of life as well as its twists and turns, he developed an eye for the underlying wonders of life and in 2018 started expressing stories, experiences and observation of human scenarios through poetry. He aspires to continue writing thought-provoking poems to dictate hidden realities.

Engelhardt Unaeb is a 34 year old composer, choir conductor and music educator from Swakopmund, currently residing in Windhoek. He writes poetry in his spare time. His inspiration to write comes from choral music. He has been commissioned to compose for Namibian choirs and often struggles to find appropriate poetry to set to music.

Pedro Vorster was born in Grootfontein, Namibia in 1952. He attended Windhoek High School and matriculated in 1969, obtained a telecomunication's draftsperson certificate in 1976 and a BA degree, UNISA, in 1980. Pedro started at NamPower in 1980 and went on pension as Civil Projects Superintendent after 37 years of service. During this time he became involved in the visual arts and acted as freelance art editor of the *Windhoek Observer* newspaper in the late eighties for nearly seven years. He also wrote satirical sketches for *The Namibian* newspaper. His published works include *Headfull* (Macmillan, 2012), a book of short satirical essays.

Printed in the United States
By Bookmasters